Y0-ASM-432

JAMESTOWN EDUCATION

Timed Readings Plus
in Social Studies

BOOK 7

**25 Two-Part Lessons with Questions for
Building Reading Speed and Comprehension**

Mc Graw Hill **Glencoe**

New York, New York   Columbus, Ohio   Chicago, Illinois   Peoria, Illinois   Woodland Hills, California

JAMESTOWN EDUCATION

Glencoe

The McGraw·Hill Companies

ISBN: 0-07-845805-6

Copyright © 2003 The McGraw-Hill Companies, Inc. All rights reserved. Except as permitted under the United States Copyright Act, no part of this publication may be reproduced or distributed in any form or by any means, or stored in a database or retrieval system, without prior written permission of the publisher.

Send all queries to:
Glencoe/McGraw-Hill
8787 Orion Place
Columbus, OH 43240-4027

2 3 4 5 6 7 8 9 10 021 08 07 06 05 04

CONTENTS

To the Student

You probably talk at an average rate of about 150 words a minute. If you are a reader of average ability, you read at a rate of about 250 words a minute. So your reading speed is nearly twice as fast as your speaking or listening speed. This example shows that reading is one of the fastest ways to get information.

The purpose of this book is to help you increase your reading rate and understand what you read. The 25 lessons in this book will also give you practice in reading social studies articles and in preparing for tests in which you must read and understand nonfiction passages within a certain time limit.

Reading Faster and Better

Following are some strategies that you can use to read the articles in each lesson.

Previewing

Previewing before you read is a very important step. This helps you to get an idea of what a selection is about and to recall any previous knowledge you have about the subject. Here are the steps to follow when previewing.

Read the title. Titles are designed not only to announce the subject but also to make the reader think. Ask yourself questions such as What can I learn from the title? What thoughts does it bring to mind?

What do I already know about this subject?

Read the first sentence. If they are short, read the first two sentences. The opening sentence is the writer's opportunity to get your attention. Some writers announce what they hope to tell you in the selection. Some writers state their purpose for writing; others just try to get your attention.

Read the last sentence. If it is short, read the final two sentences. The closing sentence is the writer's last chance to get ideas across to you. Some writers repeat the main idea once more. Some writers draw a conclusion—this is what they have been leading up to. Other writers summarize their thoughts; they tie all the facts together.

Skim the entire selection. Glance through the selection quickly to see what other information you can pick up. Look for anything that will help you read fluently and with understanding. Are there names, dates, or numbers? If so, you may have to read more slowly.

Reading for Meaning

Here are some ways to make sure you are making sense of what you read.

Build your concentration. You cannot understand what you read if you are not concentrating. When you discover that your thoughts are straying, correct the situation right away. Avoid distractions and distracting situations. Keep in mind the information you learned from previewing. This will help focus your attention on the selection.

Read in thought groups. Try to see meaningful combinations of words—phrases, clauses, or sentences. If you look at only one word at a time (called word-by-word reading), both your comprehension and your reading speed suffer.

Ask yourself questions. To sustain the pace you have set for yourself and to maintain a high level of concentration and comprehension, ask yourself questions such as What does this mean? or How can I use this information? as you read.

Finding the Main Ideas

The paragraph is the basic unit of meaning. If you can quickly discover and understand the main idea of each paragraph, you will build your comprehension of the selection.

Find the topic sentence. The topic sentence, which contains the main idea, often is the first sentence of a paragraph. It is followed by sentences that support, develop, or explain the main idea. Sometimes a topic sentence comes at the end of a paragraph. When it does, the supporting details come first, building the base for the topic sentence. Some paragraphs do not have a topic sentence; all of the sentences combine to create a meaningful idea.

Understand paragraph structure. Every well-written paragraph has a purpose. The purpose may be to inform, define, explain, or illustrate. The purpose should always relate to the main idea and expand on it. As you read each paragraph, see how the body of the paragraph tells you more about the main idea.

Relate ideas as you read. As you read the selection, notice how the writer puts together ideas. As you discover the relationship between the ideas, the main ideas come through quickly and clearly.

Mastering Reading Comprehension

Reading fast is not useful if you don't remember or understand what you read. The two exercises in Part A provide a check on how well you have understood the article.

Recalling Facts

These multiple-choice questions provide a quick check to see how well you recall important information from the article. As you learn to apply the reading strategies described earlier, you should be able to answer these questions more successfully.

Understanding Ideas

These questions require you to think about the main ideas in the article. Some main ideas are stated in the article; others are not. To answer some of the questions, you need to draw conclusions about what you read.

The five exercises in Part B require multiple answers. These exercises provide practice in applying comprehension and critical thinking skills that you can use in all your reading.

Recognizing Words in Context

Always check to see whether the words around an unfamiliar word—its context—can give you a clue to the word's meaning. A word generally appears in a context related to its meaning.

Suppose, for example, that you are unsure of the meaning of the word *expired* in the following passage:

> Vera wanted to check out a book, but her library card had expired. She had to borrow my card, because she didn't have time to renew hers.

You could begin to figure out the meaning of *expired* by asking yourself a question such as, What could have happened to Vera's library card that would make her need to borrow someone else's card? You might realize that if Vera had to renew her card, its usefulness must have come to an end or run out. This would lead you to conclude that the word *expired* must mean "to come to an end" or "to run out." You would be right. The context suggested the meaning.

Context can also affect the meaning of a word you already know. The word *key,* for instance, has many meanings. There are musical keys, door keys, and keys to solving a mystery. The context in which the word *key* occurs will tell you which meaning is correct.

Sometimes a word is explained by the words that immediately follow it. The subject of a sentence and your knowledge about that subject might also help you determine the meaning of an unknown word. Try to decide the meaning of the word *revive* in the following sentence:

> Sunshine and water will revive those drooping plants.

The compound subject is *sunshine* and *water*. You know that plants need light and water to survive and that drooping plants are not healthy. You can figure out that *revive* means "to bring back to health."

Distinguishing Fact from Opinion

Every day you are called upon to sort out fact and opinion. Because much of what you read and hear contains both facts and opinions, you need to be able to tell the two apart.

Facts are statements that can be proved. The proof must be objective and verifiable. You must be able to check for yourself to confirm a fact.

Look at the following facts. Notice that they can be checked for accuracy and confirmed. Suggested sources for verification appear in parentheses.

- Abraham Lincoln was the 16th president of the United States. (Consult biographies, social studies books, encyclopedias, and similar sources.)

- Earth revolves around the Sun. (Research in encyclopedias or astronomy books; ask knowledgeable people.)
- Dogs walk on four legs. (See for yourself.)

Opinions are statements that cannot be proved. There is no objective evidence you can consult to check the truthfulness of an opinion. Unlike facts, opinions express personal beliefs or judgments. Opinions reveal how someone feels about a subject, not the facts about that subject. You might agree or disagree with someone's opinion, but you cannot prove it right or wrong.

Look at the following opinions. The reasons these statements are classified as opinions appear in parentheses.

- Abraham Lincoln was born to be a president. (You cannot prove this by referring to birth records. There is no evidence to support this belief.)

- Earth is the only planet in our solar system where intelligent life exists. (There is no proof of this. It may be proved true some day, but for now it is just an educated guess—not a fact.)

- The dog is a human's best friend. (This is not a fact; your best friend might not be a dog.)

As you read, be aware that facts and opinions are often mixed together. Both are useful to you as a reader. But to evaluate what you read and to read intelligently, you need to know the difference between the two.

Keeping Events in Order

Sequence, or chronological order, is the order of events in a story or article or the order of steps in a process. Paying attention to the sequence of events or steps will help you follow what is happening, predict what might happen next, and make sense of a passage.

To make the sequence as clear as possible, writers often use signal words to help the reader get a more exact idea of when things happen. Following is a list of frequently used signal words and phrases:

until	first
next	then
before	after
finally	later
when	while
during	now
at the end	by the time
as soon as	in the beginning

Signal words and phrases are also useful when a writer chooses to relate details or events out of sequence. You need to pay careful attention to determine the correct chronological order.

Making Correct Inferences

Much of what you read *suggests* more than it *says*. Writers often do not state ideas directly in a text. They can't. Think of the time and space it would take to state every idea. And think of how boring that would be! Instead, writers leave it to you, the reader, to fill in the information they leave out—to make inferences. You do this by combining clues in the story or article with knowledge from your own experience.

You make many inferences every day. Suppose, for example, that you are visiting a friend's house for the first time. You see a bag of kitty litter. You infer (make an inference) that the family has a cat. Another day you overhear a conversation. You catch the names of two actors and the words *scene, dialogue,* and *directing*. You infer that the people are discussing a movie or play.

In these situations and others like them, you infer unstated information from what you observe or read. Readers must make inferences in order to understand text.

Be careful about the inferences you make. One set of facts may suggest several inferences. Some of these inferences could be faulty. A correct inference must be supported by evidence.

Remember that bag of kitty litter that caused you to infer that your friend has a cat? That could be a faulty inference. Perhaps your friend's family uses the kitty litter on their icy sidewalks to create traction. To be sure your inference is correct, you need more evidence.

Understanding Main Ideas

The main idea is the most important idea in a paragraph or passage—the idea that provides purpose and direction. The rest of the selection explains, develops, or supports the main idea. Without a main idea, there would be only a collection of unconnected thoughts.

In the following paragraph, the main idea is printed in italics. As you read, observe how the other sentences develop or explain the main idea.

Typhoon Chris hit with full fury today on the central coast of Japan. Heavy rain from the storm flooded the area. High waves carried many homes into the sea. People now fear that the heavy rains will cause mudslides in the central part of the country. The number of people killed by the storm may climb past the 200 mark by Saturday.

In this paragraph, the main-idea statement appears first. It is followed by sentences that explain, support, or give details. Sometimes the main idea appears at the end of a paragraph. Writers often put the main idea at the end of a paragraph when their purpose is to persuade or convince. Readers may be more open to a new idea if the reasons for it are presented first.

As you read the following paragraph, think about the overall impact of the supporting ideas. Their purpose is to convince the reader that the main idea in the last sentence should be accepted.

Last week there was a head-on collision at Huntington and Canton streets. Just a month ago a pedestrian was struck there. Fortunately, she was only slightly injured. In the past year, there have been more accidents there than at any other corner in the city. In fact, nearly 10 percent of all accidents in the city occur at the corner. This intersection is very dangerous, and a traffic signal should be installed there before a life is lost.

The details in the paragraph progress from least important to most important. They achieve their full effect in the main idea statement at the end.

In many cases, the main idea is not expressed in a single sentence. The reader is called upon to interpret all of the ideas expressed in the paragraph and to decide upon a main idea. Read the following paragraph.

> The American author Jack London was once a pupil at the Cole Grammar School in Oakland, California. Each morning the class sang a song. When the teacher noticed that Jack wouldn't sing, she sent him to the principal. He returned to class with a note. The note said that Jack could be excused from singing with the class if he would write an essay every morning.

In this paragraph, the reader has to interpret the individual ideas and to decide on a main idea. This main idea seems reasonable: Jack London's career as a writer began with a punishment in grammar school.

Understanding the concept of the main idea and knowing how to find it is important. Transferring that understanding to your reading and study is also important.

Working Through a Lesson

Part A

1. **Preview the article.** Locate the timed selection in Part A of the lesson that you are going to read. Wait for your teacher's signal to preview. You will have 20 seconds for previewing. Follow the previewing steps described on page 2.

2. **Read the article.** When your teacher gives you the signal, begin reading. Read carefully so that you will be able to answer questions about what you have read. When you finish reading, look at the board and note your reading time. Write this time at the bottom of the page on the line labeled Reading Time.

3. **Complete the exercises.** Answer the 10 questions that follow the article. There are 5 fact questions and 5 idea questions. Choose the best answer to each question and put an X in that box.

4. **Correct your work.** Use the Answer Key at the back of the book to check your answers. Circle any wrong answer and put an X in the box you should have marked. Record the number of correct answers on the appropriate line at the end of the lesson.

Part B

1. **Preview and read the passage.** Use the same techniques you

used to read Part A. Think about what you are reading.

2. **Complete the exercises.** Instructions are given for answering each category of question. There are 15 responses for you to record.

3. **Correct your work.** Use the Answer Key at the back of the book. Circle any wrong answer and write the correct letter or number next to it. Record the number of correct answers on the appropriate line at the end of the lesson.

Plotting Your Progress

1. **Find your reading rate.** Turn to the Reading Rate graph on page 116. Put an X at the point where the vertical line that represents the lesson intersects your reading time, shown along the left-hand side. The right-hand side of the graph will reveal your words-per-minute reading speed.

2. **Find your comprehension score.** Add your scores for Part A and Part B to determine your total number of correct answers. Turn to the Comprehension Score Graph on page 117. Put an X at the point where the vertical line that represents your lesson intersects your total correct answers, shown along the left-hand side. The right-hand side of the graph will show the percentage of questions you answered correctly.

3. **Complete the Comprehension Skills Profile.** Turn to page 118. Record your incorrect answers for the Part B exercises. The five Part B skills are listed along the bottom. There are five columns of boxes, one column for each question. For every incorrect answer, put an X in a box for that skill.

To get the most benefit from these lessons, you need to take charge of your own progress in improving your reading speed and comprehension. Studying these graphs will help you to see whether your reading rate is increasing and to determine what skills you need to work on. Your teacher will also review the graphs to check your progress.

TO THE TEACHER

About the Series

Timed Readings Plus in Social Studies includes 10 books at reading levels 4–13, with one book at each level. Book One contains material at a fourth-grade reading level; Book Two at a fifth-grade level, and so on. The readability level is determined by the Fry Readability Scale and is not to be confused with grade or age level of the student. The books are designed for use with students at middle school level and above.

The purposes of the series are as follows:

- to provide systematic, structured reading practice that helps students improve their reading rate and comprehension skills

- to give students practice in reading and understanding informational articles in the content area of social studies

- to give students experience in reading various text types—informational, expository, narrative, and prescriptive

- to prepare students for taking standardized tests that include timed reading passages in various content areas

- to provide materials with a wide range of reading levels so that students can continue to practice and improve their reading rate and comprehension skills

Because the books are designed for use with students at designated reading levels rather than in a particular grade, the social studies topics in this series are not correlated to any grade-level curriculum. Most standardized tests require students to read and comprehend social studies passages. This series provides an opportunity for students to become familiar with the particular requirements of reading social studies. For example, the vocabulary in a social studies article is important. Students need to know certain words in order to understand the concepts and the information.

Each book in the series contains 25 two-part lessons. Part A focuses on improving reading rate. This section of the lesson consists of a 400-word timed informational article on a social studies topic followed by two multiple-choice exercises. Recalling Facts includes five fact questions; Understanding Ideas includes five critical thinking questions.

Part B concentrates on building mastery in critical areas of comprehension. This section consists of a nontimed passage—the "plus" passage—followed by five exercises that address five major comprehension skills. The passage varies in length; its subject matter relates to the content of the timed selection.

Timed Reading and Comprehension

Timed reading is the best-known method of improving reading speed. There is no point in someone's reading at an accelerated speed if the person does not understand what she or he is reading. Nothing is more important than comprehension in reading. The main purpose of reading is to gain knowledge and insight, to understand the information that the writer and the text are communicating.

Few students will be able to read a passage once and answer all of the questions correctly. A score of 70 or 80 percent correct is normal. If the student gets 90 or 100 percent correct, he or she is either reading too slowly or the material is at too low a reading level. A comprehension or critical thinking score of less than 70 percent indicates a need for improvement.

One method of improving comprehension and critical thinking skills is for the student to go back and study each incorrect answer. First, the student should reread the question carefully. It is surprising how many students get the wrong answer simply because they have not read the question carefully. Then the student should look back in the passage to find the place where the question is answered, reread that part of the passage, and think about how to arrive at the correct answer. It is important to be able to recognize a correct answer when it is embedded in the text. Teacher guidance or class discussion will help the student find an answer.

Speed Versus Comprehension

It is not unusual for comprehension scores to decline as reading rate increases during the early weeks of timed readings. If this happens, students should attempt to level off their speed—but not lower it—and concentrate more on comprehension. Usually, if students maintain the higher speed and concentrate on comprehension, scores will gradually improve and within a week or two be back up to normal levels of 70 to 80 percent.

It is important to achieve a proper balance between speed and comprehension. An inefficient reader typically reads everything at one speed, usually slowly. Some poor readers, however, read rapidly but without satisfactory comprehension. It is important to achieve a balance between speed and comprehension. The practice that this series provides enables students to increase their reading speed while maintaining normal levels of comprehension.

Getting Started

As a rule, the passages in a book designed to improve reading speed should be relatively easy. The student should not have much difficulty with the vocabulary or the subject matter. Don't worry about the passages being too easy; students should see how quickly and efficiently they can read a passage.

Begin by assigning students to a level. A student should start with a book that is one level below his or her current reading level. If a student's reading level is not known, a suitable starting point would be one or two levels below the student's present grade in school.

Introduce students to the contents and format of the book they are using. Examine the book to see how it is organized. Talk about the parts of each lesson. Discuss the purpose of timed reading and the use of the progress graphs at the back of the book.

Timing the Reading

One suggestion for timing the reading is to have all students begin reading the selection at the same time. After one minute, write on the board the time that has elapsed and begin updating it at 10-second intervals (1:00, 1:10, 1:20, etc.). Another option is to have individual students time themselves with a stopwatch.

Teaching a Lesson

Part A

1. Give students the signal to begin previewing the lesson. Allow 20 seconds, then discuss special terms or vocabulary that students found.

2. Use one of the methods described above to time students as they read the passage. (Include the 20-second preview time as part of the first minute.) Tell students to write down the last time shown on the board or the stopwatch when they finish reading. Have them record the time in the designated space after the passage.

3. Next, have students complete the exercises in Part A. Work with them to check their answers, using the Answer Key that begins on page 114. Have them circle incorrect answers, mark the correct answers, and then record the numbers of correct answers for Part A on the appropriate line at the end of the lesson. Correct responses to eight or more questions indicate satisfactory comprehension and recall.

Part B

1. Have students read the Part B passage and complete the exercises that follow it. Directions are provided with each exercise. Correct responses require deliberation and discrimination.

2. Work with students to check their answers. Then discuss the answers with them and have them record the number of correct answers for Part B at the end of the lesson.

Have students study the correct answers to the questions they answered incorrectly. It is important that they understand why a particular answer is correct or incorrect.

Have them reread relevant parts of a passage to clarify an answer. An effective cooperative activity is to have students work in pairs to discuss their answers, explain why they chose the answers they did, and try to resolve differences.

Monitoring Progress

Have students find their total correct answers for the lesson and record their reading time and scores on the graphs on pages 116 and 117. Then have them complete the Comprehension Skills Profile on page 118. For each incorrect response to a question in Part B, students should mark an X in the box above each question type.

The legend on the Reading Rate graph automatically converts reading times to words-per-minute rates. The Comprehension Score graph automatically converts the raw scores to percentages.

These graphs provide a visual record of a student's progress. This record gives the student and you an opportunity to evaluate the student's progress and to determine the types of exercises and skills he or she needs to concentrate on.

Diagnosis and Evaluation

The following are typical reading rates.

Slow Reader—150 Words Per Minute

Average Reader—250 Words Per Minute

Fast Reader—350 Words Per Minute

A student who consistently reads at an average or above-average rate (with satisfactory comprehension) is ready to advance to the next book in the series.

A column of Xs in the Comprehension Skills Profile indicates a specific comprehension weakness. Using the profile, you can assess trends in student performance and suggest remedial work if necessary.

Benjamin Banneker: Man of Many Talents

Benjamin Banneker, scientist and inventor, was a free African American. He was born in 1731 on his family's tobacco farm near Baltimore, Maryland. His mother, Mary, was a free woman, and his father, Robert, was an enslaved African American whom Mary had bought. His grandmother, a free woman who was a former indentured servant from England, had married a slave named Banna Ka. That name was later changed to Bannaky and then to Banneker when Benjamin was in school.

When Banneker was growing up, public education was not readily available to African Americans. His grandmother taught him to read. Later he learned to write and studied mathematics at a Quaker school.

Banneker began to show signs of having extraordinary talent when he was still a young man. In 1753 he built the first striking clock in America. He dismantled a pocket watch to see how it worked and then built wooden copies of its parts. He even included hand-carved gears. The clock kept perfect time for 40 years.

As an adult, Banneker lived in a cabin he built. He borrowed books and equipment from neighbors and taught himself astronomy and advanced mathematics. He even had a skylight in his cabin to help him study the skies. In 1789 Banneker predicted a solar eclipse.

Banneker put his skills to work when he published a series of almanacs in the 1790s. These almanacs included information, based on his calculations, about weather and eclipses. In 1792 he sent the manuscript for his first almanac to Secretary of State (later President) Thomas Jefferson, who had a keen interest in science. The two men began to correspond. Jefferson (a slaveholder) and Banneker (the son of an enslaved African American) discussed how the abilities of African Americans and whites differed.

Perhaps Banneker's most visible legacy may be seen in the layout of Washington, D.C. In 1791 Banneker became part of the team that was designing the new capital city. American soldier and architect Pierre L'Enfant headed the project. Shortly after the initial plans were surveyed and drawn, L'Enfant left the project and took his drawings with him. To keep the project moving, Banneker re-created the team's proposed layout from memory—an amazing feat that took him only two days.

Benjamin Banneker accomplished many feats as a mathematician, an astronomer, and an inventor. He also used his reputation to push for social reforms, including racial equality and peace.

Reading Time _____

Recalling Facts

1. The relative of Banneker's who was an indentured servant was
   - ❑ a. his father.
   - ❑ b. his grandmother.
   - ❑ c. his mother.

2. Banneker first learned mathematics
   - ❑ a. in a Quaker school.
   - ❑ b. from his grandmother.
   - ❑ c. on his own.

3. Banneker built a wooden clock when he was
   - ❑ a. a child.
   - ❑ b. a young man.
   - ❑ c. an old man.

4. Banneker sent his first almanac to
   - ❑ a. George Washington.
   - ❑ b. Pierre L'Enfant.
   - ❑ c. Thomas Jefferson.

5. Banneker published his almanacs
   - ❑ a. in the 1790s.
   - ❑ b. in the 1770s.
   - ❑ c. in the 1730s.

Understanding Ideas

6. From reading the passage, one can conclude that a child would be free
   - ❑ a. only if both parents were free.
   - ❑ b. if his mother was free.
   - ❑ c. if his father was free.

7. Banneker's work on the design of Washington, D.C., showed his skills as
   - ❑ a. a surveyor.
   - ❑ b. an astronomer.
   - ❑ c. an inventor.

8. One can conclude from the passage that Quakers
   - ❑ a. were willing to educate African Americans.
   - ❑ b. would teach only boys.
   - ❑ c. did not place much importance on education.

9. In publishing his almanacs, Banneker demonstrated knowledge of
   - ❑ a. building clocks.
   - ❑ b. the cycles of the sun and moon.
   - ❑ c. city planning.

10. From the passage, one might infer that Benjamin Banneker and Thomas Jefferson had different ideas about
    - ❑ a. farming.
    - ❑ b. city planning.
    - ❑ c. slavery.

The Education of Free Blacks in Post-Revolutionary War Boston

In 1779 Thomas Jefferson first proposed a system of tax-supported public education. Although the plan failed, it became the basis for a system of public education that came about in the 1840s. Before then opportunities for schooling usually went to boys from wealthy families, funded by private or religious groups.

Boston's free black community saw the need to take care of its children. In 1787 Prince Hall, a prominent African American, asked the state to start a school for black children. They denied both this request and later petitions. Hall then opened his own school in his home in 1798. Ten years later, he moved the school to the local African Meeting House.

In the 1820s, schooling for African American children improved when authorities in Boston started two free schools for them. Then, in 1834, the first school in the country that was just for African American children was built. It was named after white businessman Abiel Smith. Smith had left $2,000 in his will for the education of black children.

In the late 1840s, some African American parents sued unsuccessfully to compel public schools to admit their children. The courts ruled that the parents' lawyers had not proved that the Smith School was inferior to public schools. Segregation—racial separation—was not outlawed in Massachusetts public schools until 1855.

1. Recognizing Words in Context

Find the word *inferior* in the passage. One definition below is closest to the meaning of that word. One definition has the opposite or nearly the opposite meaning. The remaining definition has a completely different meaning. Label the definitions C for *closest,* O for *opposite or nearly opposite,* and D for *different.*

_____ a. older

_____ b. better

_____ c. worse

2. Distinguishing Fact from Opinion

Two of the statements below present *facts,* which can be proved. The other statement is an *opinion,* which expresses someone's thoughts or beliefs. Label the statements F for *fact* and O for *opinion.*

_____ a. Abiel Smith was a business-man.

_____ b. The Smith School was as good as public schools.

_____ c. The Abiel Smith School was built in 1834.

3. Keeping Events in Order

Number the statements below 1, 2, and 3 to show the order in which the events took place.

_____ a. Segregation was outlawed in Massachusetts public schools.

_____ b. A school was established in the African Meeting House.

_____ c. The Smith School was built.

4. Making Correct Inferences

Two of the statements below are correct *inferences,* or reasonable guesses. They are based on information in the passage. The other statement is an incorrect, or faulty, inference. Label the statements C for *correct* inference and F for *faulty* inference.

_____ a. Before 1855, Boston public schools could refuse to admit African Americans.

_____ b. Girls generally received less education than boys in early nineteenth-century America.

_____ c. The Smith School admitted only boys.

5. Understanding Main Ideas

One of the statements below expresses the main idea of the passage. One statement is too general, or too broad. The other explains only part of the passage; it is too narrow. Label the statements M for *main idea,* B for *too broad,* and N for *too narrow.*

_____ a. Education was important to African Americans in nineteenth-century America.

_____ b. Education for Boston's African American children improved in the first half of the nineteenth century.

_____ c. The Smith School was established in 1834.

Correct Answers, Part A _____

Correct Answers, Part B _____

Total Correct Answers _____

Experiencing the Gold Rush

In 1848 a few men building a sawmill in California discovered gold. By 1849 many people, mostly men, had left their homes and flocked to California to search for the precious metal or set up businesses. Although most of the prospectors, called forty-niners, were from the United States, some came from Mexico, Chile, China, and other countries. All of them hoped to become rich.

Many city folk who searched for gold in California were unaccustomed to manual labor. Their dreams of riches shattered when, after months or even years of hard work, they found little or no gold. Some of their letters home described the wretched working conditions they endured and their longing for loved ones. Disappointment often led to resentment of competitors, especially when those who were successful were foreigners.

Many Mexicans and Chileans had been miners before coming to California. Their knowledge and experience helped them. This, in turn, made them the target of attacks by American miners. In 1850 the California legislature approved a tax on all foreign miners. Although some paid the tax and kept searching for gold, many others left California or stopped mining.

Some of the most successful miners were Chinese immigrants. Many had been farmers in China and hoped to find enough gold to pay off debts. Others had been miners. They were used to hard work—and, as they usually worked in large groups, they could work more efficiently than one person alone. They often took over claims abandoned by American miners, yet still they managed to find enough gold dust to eke out a profit.

As resentment against foreigners grew, many Chinese were beaten or their mining camps destroyed. Some returned to China. Others opened businesses. Because few women had journeyed to California, there were opportunities to do jobs that women traditionally did, such as washing clothes or cooking. Some Chinese who opened laundries or restaurants became wealthy.

African Americans also mined for gold during the Gold Rush, but not all of them were free. California had become a state in 1850 and did not allow slavery, but the practice was still legal in other states. Some slaveholders brought enslaved African Americans to California to prospect for gold. Unlike other miners, some of these African Americans wanted to find gold so that they could buy freedom for themselves and their families. Some succeeded, and in the end perhaps they gained the most valuable of all riches.

Reading Time _____

Recalling Facts

1. Most of the forty-niners were
   - ❑ a. U.S. citizens.
   - ❑ b. Chinese.
   - ❑ c. Mexicans.

2. Chinese miners usually worked
   - ❑ a. alone.
   - ❑ b. with American miners.
   - ❑ c. in large groups.

3. Many city folk who searched for gold were
   - ❑ a. unaccustomed to hard labor.
   - ❑ b. quick to give up mining.
   - ❑ c. hoping to buy their freedom.

4. In 1850 the California legislature approved
   - ❑ a. the institution of slavery.
   - ❑ b. a tax on foreign miners.
   - ❑ c. new mines.

5. Some African Americans wanted to find gold to
   - ❑ a. buy their freedom.
   - ❑ b. open restaurants.
   - ❑ c. start businesses.

Understanding Ideas

6. One can conclude from the passage that experienced miners
   - ❑ a. were less successful than inexperienced miners.
   - ❑ b. had an advantage over inexperienced miners.
   - ❑ c. were almost exclusively Americans.

7. It is likely that when American miners discovered that Chinese miners had succeeded where they had failed, American miners
   - ❑ a. were resentful.
   - ❑ b. analyzed the successful methods of the Chinese miners.
   - ❑ c. believed that they could learn from the Chinese.

8. During the Gold Rush,
   - ❑ a. most forty-niners struck it rich.
   - ❑ b. many ambitious and hard-working people found various opportunities to succeed.
   - ❑ c. most miners brought their families to the mines for companionship.

9. Unlike many African American miners, other miners
   - ❑ a. found gold.
   - ❑ b. had families.
   - ❑ c. were free.

10. It is likely that the author of the passage considers
    - ❑ a. gold worth great sacrifices.
    - ❑ b. hard work what always brings success.
    - ❑ c. freedom more important than gold.

Entrepreneurs of the Gold Rush

During the Gold Rush, many entrepreneurs did not mine for gold, yet some became fabulously wealthy. Although James Marshall tried to keep his discovery of gold at Sutter's Mill a secret, Sam Brannan, a salesman, soon heard about it and set out to make his fortune. He bought all of the mining equipment he could find. Then he advertised the discovery of gold. Soon people were flocking to Brannan's store to buy picks, shovels, and other mining equipment at his inflated prices. In less than three months' time, he had earned $36,000. By 1856, just eight years after Marshall had discovered gold, Brannan was the richest man in California.

Other enterprising people also took advantage of gold seekers. Parts of the overland route to California were devoid of drinkable water. Many unprepared travelers died of thirst. Entrepreneurs capitalized on the situation by selling water along the way, sometimes for as much as $100 a drink.

Similarly people charged outrageous amounts of money for things that miners needed. Some made their fortunes cooking, cleaning, doing laundry, running hotels, or lending money during the Gold Rush.

In 1853 Levi Strauss established a dry goods business in San Francisco. He sold supplies to miners and made a fortune. However, today he is best remembered for the jeans that his company started making after the Gold Rush.

1. **Recognizing Words in Context**

   Find the word *devoid* in the passage. One definition below is closest to the meaning of that word. One definition has the opposite or nearly the opposite meaning. The remaining definition has a completely different meaning. Label the definitions C for *closest,* O for *opposite or nearly opposite,* and D for *different.*

   _____ a. prepared

   _____ b. empty

   _____ c. full

2. **Distinguishing Fact from Opinion**

   Two of the statements below present *facts,* which can be proved. The other statement is an *opinion,* which expresses someone's thoughts or beliefs. Label the statements F for *fact* and O for *opinion.*

   _____ a. Sam Brannan was the most opportunistic entrepreneur of the Gold Rush.

   _____ b. Sam Brannan sold mining equipment at a great profit.

   _____ c. Sam Brannan was one of many successful Gold Rush entrepreneurs.

3. Keeping Events in Order

Number the statements below 1, 2, and 3 to show the order in which the events took place.

_____ a. Brannan heard that gold was discovered at Sutter's Mill.

_____ b. Brannan sold mining equipment.

_____ c. Brannan bought mining equipment.

4. Making Correct Inferences

Two of the statements below are correct *inferences,* or reasonable guesses. They are based on information in the passage. The other statement is an incorrect, or faulty, inference. Label the statements C for *correct* inference and F for *faulty* inference.

_____ a. Entrepreneurs want to make money.

_____ b. Entrepreneurs are interested in making money but are never interested in helping others.

_____ c. Successful entrepreneurs take advantage of opportunities to make money.

5. Understanding Main Ideas

One of the statements below expresses the main idea of the passage. One statement is too general, or too broad. The other explains only part of the passage; it is too narrow. Label the statements M for *main idea,* B for *too broad,* and N for *too narrow.*

_____ a. Many people traveled west to make money.

_____ b. Brannan became the wealthiest man in California.

_____ c. Entrepreneurs who provided desirable goods and services could make money during the Gold Rush.

Correct Answers, Part A _____

Correct Answers, Part B _____

Total Correct Answers _____

3   A   Lives of the Shakers

The Shakers are a religious sect that flourished in the United States between the time of the American Revolution and the first half of the nineteenth century. They were most commonly found in New York, New England, and the frontier areas of Kentucky and Ohio.

The Shakers have been described as *millenarian* because of their belief that Christ's Second Coming would usher in 1,000 years of peace. They were first known as the Shaking Quakers. The name came about as a result of the extreme trembling that they exhibited during their ecstatic dancing and singing in their worship services.

Shakers followed an extremely simple communal lifestyle. They held all property in common. Men and women shared equally in the work and governance of the community. The spare design of their buildings and furniture, their old-fashioned clothing, and their unfashionable hairstyles reflected their emphasis on the spiritual rather than the material.

The community was organized into families. A Shaker family was larger than a typical nuclear family. Elders, deacons, and trustees, both male and female, were the heads of each family. Each family had its own dormitory, cooking and eating areas, barns, and work areas. Younger members might be engaged in outdoor or indoor tasks, depending on their abilities as farmers or artisans. Older members and those who had previously been married were most likely to be engaged in the business aspects of the community.

The main belief that distinguished Shakers from mainstream Protestants was their practice of celibacy. Men and women lived in separate dormitories. The Shaker sect grew by converting adults and rearing orphans. As adults the orphans could choose whether to stay with the community.

Hard work was as important in the Shakers' relationship to God as were formal worship services. The Shakers engaged in farming and related activities such as sheep herding and raising bees. They also made simple furniture and craft items for sale. They used the proceeds to buy land.

Although many people admired their prosperous farms, functional furniture, and simple building style, the Shakers' ecstatic worship and their practice of holding seances aroused suspicion among mainstream Christians. Shakers reached the peak of their membership (about 6,000) right before the Civil War. After that, their membership declined, and after 1965 they accepted no new members. Today only a few elderly women live in a Shaker community in Maine.

Reading Time _____

Recalling Facts

1. The first Shaker community in the United States was established just after the
   - ❑ a. American Revolution.
   - ❑ b. Civil War.
   - ❑ c. Pilgrims at Plymouth Plantation.

2. Shaker worship was characterized by
   - ❑ a. long sermons.
   - ❑ b. ecstatic singing and dancing.
   - ❑ c. sitting together in silence.

3. A Shaker family was _____ a traditional nuclear family.
   - ❑ a. larger than
   - ❑ b. smaller than
   - ❑ c. the same size as

4. Shaker membership peaked in the _____ century.
   - ❑ a. eighteenth
   - ❑ b. nineteenth
   - ❑ c. twentieth

5. Shakers had communities in
   - ❑ a. Pennsylvania.
   - ❑ b. Kentucky.
   - ❑ c. Virginia.

Understanding Ideas

6. From reading the passage, one can conclude that the Shakers
   - ❑ a. were a relatively small denomination.
   - ❑ b. were once larger than most mainstream Protestant groups.
   - ❑ c. lived in poverty.

7. Given the Shaker style of life and governance, one might expect Shakers to
   - ❑ a. concentrate authority in a single individual.
   - ❑ b. support equal rights for women.
   - ❑ c. amass personal fortunes.

8. From the passage, one can conclude that the Shaker lifestyle
   - ❑ a. was similar to the lifestyle of most other Protestants.
   - ❑ b. was sometimes difficult to adhere to.
   - ❑ c. appealed only to older people.

9. The main idea of this passage is that
   - ❑ a. Shakers made beautiful furniture.
   - ❑ b. the Shaker sect was characterized by simplicity and a communal lifestyle.
   - ❑ c. Shakers flourished before the Civil War.

10. One may infer that the primary motivation for everything the Shakers did was
    - ❑ a. artistic.
    - ❑ b. practical.
    - ❑ c. spiritual.

3   B   Mother Ann Lee

Ann Lee was born in Manchester, England, in 1736. A poor, illiterate young textile worker, she married a blacksmith and had four children, all of whom died young. From an early age, Lee exhibited great piety; at the age of 22, she joined a new religious group known as the Shaking Quakers. While in prison for observing her religious practices, she experienced spiritual visions and trances. She became convinced that she was Christ, whose Second Coming had been foretold, in female form. A small group of followers, including her husband, acknowledged her as their leader in 1772 and began to refer to her as Mother Ann.

One of Mother Ann's visions led her to escape further persecution by coming to the United States. In 1776, near Albany, New York, Mother Ann and her followers established the first Shaker farming community. Mother Ann's husband had by this time abandoned her. Perhaps as a result of this experience and the early deaths of her children, Mother Ann preached the doctrine of celibacy. Being charismatic, she attracted converts from other congregations, many of whom had experienced conversion but were unsure how to put their faith to work.

Mother Ann Lee died in 1784, but the Shaker communities continued to grow for almost 80 years. Her personal writings are known as Mother's Wisdom.

1. **Recognizing Words in Context**
   Find the word *piety* in the passage. One definition below is closest to the meaning of that word. One definition has the opposite or nearly the opposite meaning. The remaining definition has a completely different meaning. Label the definitions C for *closest*, O for *opposite or nearly opposite*, and D for *different*.

   _____ a. holiness

   _____ b. irreverence

   _____ c. playfulness

2. **Distinguishing Fact from Opinion**
   Two of the statements below present *facts*, which can be proved. The other statement is an *opinion*, which expresses someone's thoughts or beliefs. Label the statements F for *fact* and O for *opinion*.

   _____ a. Ann Lee emigrated to the United States from England.

   _____ b. Ann Lee had four children, all of whom died young.

   _____ c. Mother Ann was the most charismatic leader of her time.

3. Keeping Events in Order

Number the statements below 1, 2, and 3 to show the order in which the events took place.

_____ a. The Shakers established a farm in New York.

_____ b. The Shakers attracted converts in the United States.

_____ c. Ann Lee joined the Shaking Quakers.

4. Making Correct Inferences

Two of the statements below are correct *inferences,* or reasonable guesses. They are based on information in the passage. The other statement is an incorrect, or faulty, inference. Label the statements C for *correct* inference and F for *faulty* inference.

_____ a. The Shakers were persecuted in England for their beliefs.

_____ b. Ann Lee was interested in religion throughout her life.

_____ c. Ann Lee's personality was unimportant in attracting converts.

5. Understanding Main Ideas

One of the statements below expresses the main idea of the passage. One statement is too general, or too broad. The other explains only part of the passage; it is too narrow. Label the statements M for *main idea,* B for *too broad,* and N for *too narrow.*

_____ a. Influenced by her experiences and spiritual visions, Ann Lee was instrumental in establishing the Shaker sect.

_____ b. The Shakers are a religious group established during the eighteenth century.

_____ c. Ann Lee's visions while in prison convinced her that she was Christ, whose Second Coming had been foretold, in female form.

Correct Answers, Part A _____

Correct Answers, Part B _____

Total Correct Answers _____

These Walls Can Talk

pintura rupestre

Human beings have been painting murals on walls since they first started making art. Murals have been used to illustrate history and memorialize important people. In modern times, some murals in public locations have stirred up controversy.

cuevas

Our prehistoric ancestors produced the first-known wall paintings during the Paleolithic Period, the early Stone Age, some 30,000 years ago. Some of these murals, found deep inside caves at Lascaux, France, feature images of horses, bison, deer, mammoths, and other animals. Anthropologists believe that the murals may have been used in rituals. One possibility is that they served as requests to the gods for good hunting.

The ancient Egyptians decorated the walls of their tombs with paintings. These often showed activities of daily life, such as hunting and farming. One famous scene shows musicians and dancers at a great feast. During the Italian Renaissance, painters decorated walls with paintings called frescoes. In a church, frescoes might depict biblical stories. In private homes, they might portray family members and important events.

Many artists in the twentieth and twenty-first centuries have used murals to promote social change. In the 1920s, the Mexican government hired artists such as Diego Rivera and José Orozco to create large public murals illustrating Mexican history and promoting the ideals of the revolution of 1917. These artists also created murals in the United States that expressed their beliefs.

The mural tradition caught on among the Hispanic groups in the Southwest. Today, Los Angeles is a center for mural art. The Great Wall of Los Angeles, the world's longest mural, stretches more than 2,500 feet. This mural took six years to paint and involved more than 200 young people working under the direction of muralist Judy Baca. The mural illustrates California history.

Since the late 1980s, three painters who call themselves the Bogside Artists have created large murals in and around the city of Derry, Northern Ireland. Their works are a dramatic chronicle of the struggle of Northern Ireland's Catholics for civil rights. The murals, which are about 25 feet tall, cover the windowless sides of buildings. One of the most famous, *Petrol Bomber*, shows a young boy wearing a gas mask. It is a scene from the 1969 Battle of Bogside, in which British forces clashed with protesters.

Reading Time 1´73

Recalling Facts

1. Prehistoric cave murals have been found in
   - ❑ a. Mexico.
   - ❑ b. the U.S. Southwest.
   - ❑ c. France.

2. The tomb paintings of Egypt
   - ❑ a. provided religious inspiration for ordinary people.
   - ❑ b. showed activities of daily life, such as hunting and farming.
   - ❑ c. were used to protest against social injustice.

3. During the Italian Renaissance, painters decorated walls with paintings called
   - ❑ a. watercolors.
   - ❑ b. frescoes.
   - ❑ c. intaglios.

4. The Great Wall of Los Angeles
   - ❑ a. tells the story of Diego Rivera's life.
   - ❑ b. imitates the murals of the Italian Renaissance.
   - ❑ c. illustrates California history.

5. The murals of the Bogside Artists portray
   - ❑ a. the struggles of Northern Ireland's Catholics.
   - ❑ b. game animals.
   - ❑ c. the story of the Mexican Revolution.

Understanding Ideas

6. A likely reason that cave painters created images of animals was
   - ❑ a. to tell travelers about the wildlife of their region.
   - ❑ b. to ask their gods to make these animals plentiful.
   - ❑ c. to keep records of the animals.

7. Most mural art
   - ❑ a. portrays controversial figures.
   - ❑ b. expresses ideas important to the community.
   - ❑ c. creates disagreement.

8. Two examples of mural art with religious implications are
   - ❑ a. the works of Michelangelo and Egyptian tomb art.
   - ❑ b. the works of the Bogside Artists and ancient cave murals.
   - ❑ c. the Great Wall of Los Angeles and the murals of José Orozco.

9. The words "Our fervent wish is that the peace process will give us time to put right what has been so drastically put wrong" were most likely spoken by
   - ❑ a. an Italian Renaissance painter.
   - ❑ b. Judy Baca.
   - ❑ c. a Bogside Artist.

10. Which of the following statements best expresses the main idea?
    - ❑ a. Ancient mural art usually has a religious purpose, and modern mural art is usually political.
    - ❑ b. Throughout human history, artists have painted murals in public places to express ideas that they believed are important.
    - ❑ c. Mural art has existed for at least 30,000 years.

How to Carry Out a Public Mural Project

Any public mural project must be undertaken by considering its two main aspects—artistic and administrative.

Obtaining funding is generally the first step in the administrative process. Donations, fund-raising events, and government grants are typical sources. If the administrators of the project are not themselves artists, they must select an artist. This is often done through a competition. Calls for entries usually state the theme or topic of the mural, which has been decided by the administrators.

Once the artistic team is assembled, members prepare the wall for painting. They clean the surface and repair cracks and holes. Painters then coat the wall with *primer*, a type of paint that forms a good foundation for painting. The artist measures the wall and prepares a *maquette*, or scale drawing, that serves as a pattern. Work on the mural can now begin.

In the meantime, the administrators may be promoting the project by holding public relations events, distributing brochures and photos, and sending out press releases on the progress of the project. The work does not end with the unveiling of the mural, however. To ensure that the community can enjoy the mural for years to come, experts recommend that it be cleaned every year to protect it from damage by pollution and weather.

1. **Recognizing Words in Context**

   Find the word *administrative* in the passage. One definition below is closest to the meaning of that word. One definition has the opposite or nearly the opposite meaning. The remaining definition has a completely different meaning. Label the definitions C for *closest*, O for *opposite or nearly opposite*, and D for *different*.

   _____ a. managerial

   _____ b. out of order

   _____ c. lacking organization

2. **Distinguishing Fact from Opinion**

   Two of the statements below present *facts*, which can be proved. The other statement is an *opinion*, which expresses someone's thoughts or beliefs. Label the statements F for *fact* and O for *opinion*.

   _____ a. Artists lack the skills to be successful administrators.

   _____ b. Proper preparation of the wall helps ensure that a mural will last.

   _____ c. Holding a competition is one way of selecting an artist for a mural project.

3. Keeping Events in Order

Number the statements below 1, 2, and 3 to show the order in which the events took place.

_____ a. The mural committee holds a fund-raising event.

_____ b. The artistic team primes the wall.

_____ c. Workers clean the mural.

4. Making Correct Inferences

Two of the statements below are correct *inferences,* or reasonable guesses. They are based on information in the passage. The other statement is an incorrect, or faulty, inference. Label the statements C for *correct* inference and F for *faulty* inference.

_____ a. A mural project takes a year or more to complete.

_____ b. The support of the community is important in a mural project.

_____ c. Several types of skills or talents are needed to carry out a mural project.

5. Understanding Main Ideas

One of the statements below expresses the main idea of the passage. One statement is too general, or too broad. The other explains only part of the passage; it is too narrow. Label the statements M for *main idea,* B for *too broad,* and N for *too narrow.*

_____ a. A successful mural project involves administrative and artistic tasks.

_____ b. The wall on which a mural is painted should be free of cracks.

_____ c. A mural is a form of public art.

Correct Answers, Part A _____

Correct Answers, Part B _____

Total Correct Answers _____

What Happens to Tax Dollars?

Most people are surprised to learn how much money is deducted from their earnings. *Gross pay* is a person's total wages or salary, and *net pay* is what remains after deductions. Where does the deducted money go?

About 6 percent of each paycheck goes to Social Security, which protects the income of retired or disabled people. Workers who pay into the fund receive benefits, usually when they retire. In 2001 nearly one-third of the government's money came from Social Security and Medicare taxes.

Employers also withhold part of each check for federal income tax. This tax is the federal government's largest source of revenue. In 2001, one-half of the government's money came from taxes paid by individuals.

Taxpayers often wonder what they receive for the money taken from their paychecks. The president must answer that question every year. According to the U.S. Constitution, the president must have approval from Congress to spend money. The president prepares an annual budget that summarizes the government's income and suggests how it should be spent. Some expenses, such as veterans' benefits and interest on savings bonds, are fixed. However, the president suggests how much should be spent on discretionary expenses such as national defense or cancer research.

Circle graphs are one means the government uses to help people understand the budget. In a circle graph of federal spending, the largest part goes to Social Security; in 2001, for example, nearly one quarter of the budget (23 percent) was returned to taxpayers as Social Security payments. Another large part (19 percent) funded Medicare and Medicaid, the federal health insurance programs for the elderly and the needy. The next largest segment (16 percent) was spent on national defense. Interest paid on the public debt (13 percent) took almost as big a portion of the budget.

Americans have a right to know how their tax dollars are spent, so copies of the budget are available in print and online, but these copies contain thousands of pages. Tools such as *The Citizen's Guide to the Federal Budget* help people find the data they need. Budget Explorer, an online tutorial, allows people to compare their guesses about where their money goes to the actual numbers. Users can also try to balance the federal budget. For more details, they can visit the Web sites of different agencies. These tools are one more means of putting tax dollars to work.

Reading Time _____

Recalling Facts

1. A portion of every paycheck is withheld to fund
   - ❏ a. mortgage payments.
   - ❏ b. workers' earnings.
   - ❏ c. Social Security.

2. The main source of revenue for the federal government is
   - ❏ a. corporate tax.
   - ❏ b. individual income tax.
   - ❏ c. interest on the public debt.

3. The part of the federal budget spent on Social Security is about
   - ❏ a. 1 percent.
   - ❏ b. 10 percent.
   - ❏ c. 25 percent.

4. A budget summarizes income and
   - ❏ a. interest.
   - ❏ b. taxes.
   - ❏ c. expenses.

5. The president must submit a budget to Congress
   - ❏ a. every year.
   - ❏ b. whenever the government is in debt.
   - ❏ c. every four years.

Understanding Ideas

6. The amount of money available for programs such as cancer research is limited by
   - ❏ a. fixed expenses.
   - ❏ b. discretionary expenses.
   - ❏ c. net pay.

7. America's founders wanted government spending to be controlled by
   - ❏ a. only one branch of government.
   - ❏ b. the executive branch.
   - ❏ c. Congress and the president.

8. The budget contains the president's _____ about how tax money should be spent.
   - ❏ a. orders
   - ❏ b. recommendations
   - ❏ c. questions

9. From a circle graph of federal spending, one could infer that the government's highest priority is
   - ❏ a. national defense.
   - ❏ b. paying off the public debt.
   - ❏ c. insurance programs such as Social Security and Medicare.

10. This passage was written to
    - ❏ a. argue that less money should go to Social Security.
    - ❏ b. explain how the federal budget works.
    - ❏ c. expose wasteful government spending.

Each year people who earn money in the United States must file federal tax returns. The tax-form package includes directions for filing and a worksheet to help people decide whether they must file, but most wage earners who had taxes withheld from a paycheck must file a return.

The Internal Revenue Service (IRS) suggests that taxpayers follow certain steps to file. First, they must collect the necessary information. Interest accrued on savings accounts or other investments is reported on 1099 forms. Taxes withheld by employers are reported on W-2 forms. These forms should arrive in the mail by January 31.

Next, taxpayers must obtain tax forms for filing. Most young taxpayers can file form 1040EZ. The form is available online or at federal offices such as the U.S. Post Office.

Filling out the form should take only a few hours. Line-by-line directions are included, and the IRS provides a toll-free help line and publications to answer questions.

After completing the form, the taxpayer should sign and date it. Forms may be mailed in or filed electronically from a home computer. Some taxpayers hire a tax preparer, although this is normally not necessary with the 1040EZ form. Taxpayers who file electronically usually receive their refunds faster, if refunds are due.

1. **Recognizing Words in Context**

   Find the word *accrued* in the passage. One definition below is closest to the meaning of that word. One definition has the opposite or nearly the opposite meaning. The remaining definition has a completely different meaning. Label the definitions C for *closest,* O for *opposite or nearly opposite,* and D for *different.*

   _____ a. lost

   _____ b. enforced

   _____ c. earned

2. **Distinguishing Fact from Opinion**

   Two of the statements below present *facts,* which can be proved. The other statement is an *opinion,* which expresses someone's thoughts or beliefs. Label the statements F for *fact* and O for *opinion.*

   _____ a. W-2 forms show the amount withheld for taxes.

   _____ b. W-2 forms should arrive by January 31.

   _____ c. Filing electronically is the best way to send in a return.

3. Keeping Events in Order

Number the statements below 1, 2, and 3 to show the order in which the events take place.

_____ a. The taxpayer signs the return.

_____ b. The taxpayer gathers records such as W-2 forms.

_____ c. The taxpayer fills out the return.

4. Making Correct Inferences

Two of the statements below are correct *inferences,* or reasonable guesses. They are based on information in the passage. The other statement is an incorrect, or faulty, inference. Label the statements C for *correct* inference and F for *faulty* inference.

_____ a. Taxpayers must keep track of W-2 forms and 1099 forms.

_____ b. Tax forms are not available through the mail.

_____ c. Some taxpayers receive a refund.

5. Understanding Main Ideas

One of the statements below expresses the main idea of the passage. One statement is too general, or too broad. The other explains only part of the passage; it is too narrow. Label the statements M for *main idea*, B for *too broad*, and N for *too narrow*.

_____ a. Interest accrued on savings accounts is reported on 1099 forms.

_____ b. The steps to filing an income tax return are not difficult to follow.

_____ c. The federal government taxes personal income.

Correct Answers, Part A _____

Correct Answers, Part B _____

Total Correct Answers _____

Nazi Germany invaded Poland in September of 1939. As a result, France and Great Britain declared war on Germany, and World War II began. The Nazis, under Adolf Hitler, quickly invaded many European countries. By the summer of 1940, the island nation of Great Britain was the Nazis' only remaining unconquered enemy in Western Europe. The Germans were eager to invade Great Britain. However, they planned to destroy the British Royal Air Force (RAF) first so that it could not bomb the German navy as it transported invading forces. The result was the Battle of Britain.

The Luftwaffe—the German air force—began by bombing ports and RAF airfields. Most of the fighting, however, took place in the skies above Great Britain. The Germans hoped to lure the RAF into the open, where quick German fighter planes would shoot down the planes.

Perhaps Hitler thought that the much smaller RAF could be easily defeated. The Germans had four times as many planes as the British, yet the Battle of Britain raged for months. During the battle, the Germans lost almost three times as many aircraft as the British. On some days, the RAF fought as many as five battles. It succeeded in keeping the enemy at bay and saved the country from Nazi occupation.

The RAF, in addition to its valiant and tireless pilots, used new technology to defend Britain. During World War II, the British introduced an invention that the Germans did not have: radar. It allowed the British to identify approaching planes in all kinds of weather, at any time of day. Thus, RAF pilots could become airborne before German planes appeared overhead.

Despite the advantages that radar gave Britain, the Luftwaffe inflicted a potentially fatal series of blows when it bombed several RAF airfields around London, causing severe damage. In September of 1940, assuming that the bombing had made the RAF ineffective, the German command shifted its attention to bombing London, the capital. Germany hoped that this would force the British to surrender, but the shift in tactics gave the RAF time to recover. Soon after, it brought down about 60 Luftwaffe planes during a series of large-scale German attacks.

Realizing that it would be unable to annihilate the RAF quickly, Germany postponed the planned invasion of Great Britain and adopted other tactics aimed at conquering it. Although there was no formal German surrender, the British considered the Battle of Britain a major victory.

Reading Time _____

Recalling Facts

1. The Battle of Britain took place chiefly
   - ❑ a. in the ocean.
   - ❑ b. in the skies.
   - ❑ c. on the ground.

2. The Germans had
   - ❑ a. fewer planes than the British.
   - ❑ b. four times as many planes as the British.
   - ❑ c. just as many planes as the British.

3. Some days the RAF fought as many as
   - ❑ a. 15 battles.
   - ❑ b. 50 battles.
   - ❑ c. 5 battles.

4. The Germans lost
   - ❑ a. almost three times as many aircraft as the British.
   - ❑ b. almost three times fewer aircraft than the British.
   - ❑ c. as many aircraft as the British.

5. The British considered the Battle of Britain
   - ❑ a. their greatest defeat.
   - ❑ b. a German victory.
   - ❑ c. a British victory.

Understanding Ideas

6. One can infer from the passage that, because Great Britain is an island,
   - ❑ a. it was easy for Germany to invade by sea.
   - ❑ b. it was difficult for Germany to invade by sea.
   - ❑ c. it was desirable for Germany to invade by sea.

7. It is possible that Germany could have defeated the RAF if the Luftwaffe had
   - ❑ a. attacked only at night.
   - ❑ b. carried out raids in foggy weather.
   - ❑ c. destroyed Britain's radar system.

8. One can conclude from the passage that the German command
   - ❑ a. underestimated the fighting capacity of the RAF.
   - ❑ b. understood the fighting capacity of the RAF.
   - ❑ c. overestimated the fighting capacity of the RAF.

9. It is likely that the RAF was able to recover because
   - ❑ a. London was far away from the airfields.
   - ❑ b. Germany made a tactical error.
   - ❑ c. it took Germany a long time to decide on its next move.

10. If Britain had not had radar, it is likely that the Luftwaffe would have
    - ❑ a. destroyed many RAF planes that were on the ground.
    - ❑ b. suffered more causalities.
    - ❑ c. detected approaching planes.

Life During the Blitz

On September 7, 1940, Nazi Germany began heavy, frequent bombing of London and other cities in Great Britain. These attacks, known as the Blitz, finally ended in May of 1941, but during the Blitz the lives of the British people changed dramatically.

At night people followed blackout regulations because light might have made them targets for German bombers. They pulled black curtains over their windows so that no light could be seen from outside and made special covers for headlights and flashlights to focus narrow beams downward. The British government issued gas masks to everyone, even babies. People carried gas masks with them everywhere.

Many people constructed air-raid shelters in their backyards; others hid in cellars or closets during an air attack. London also had hundreds of public air-raid shelters, many in underground subway stations. When an air-raid siren sounded, people went to the nearest shelter and remained there until they heard the all-clear signal and could come out. Bombs often demolished entire neighborhoods during an attack.

During the war, many goods, such as butter, were in short supply. The government rationed those items, and everyone received a specified quantity. People mended clothes or sewed new clothes from old fabric. Despite terror and hardships, the British people found courage to endure the Blitz and the war—and so to prevail.

1. Recognizing Words in Context

Find the word *rationed* in the passage. One definition below is closest to the meaning of that word. One definition has the opposite or nearly the opposite meaning. The remaining definition has a completely different meaning. Label the definitions C for *closest*, O for *opposite or nearly opposite*, and D for *different*.

_____ a. rated

_____ b. portioned

_____ c. unregulated

2. Distinguishing Fact from Opinion

Two of the statements below present *facts*, which can be proved. The other statement is an *opinion*, which expresses someone's thoughts or beliefs. Label the statements F for *fact* and O for *opinion*.

_____ a. The government issued gas masks to babies.

_____ b. The Blitz was the most terrifying period in British history.

_____ c. London had air-raid shelters in underground subway stations.

3. Keeping Events in Order

Number the statements below 1, 2, and 3 to show the order in which the events took place.

_____ a. Germany initiated the Blitz.

_____ b. People hid in air-raid shelters.

_____ c. Events changed in May of 1941.

4. Making Correct Inferences

Two of the statements below are correct *inferences,* or reasonable guesses. They are based on information in the passage. The other statement is an incorrect, or faulty, inference. Label the statements C for *correct* inference and F for *faulty* inference.

_____ a. The British were afraid that the Germans would use deadly gases in an attack.

_____ b. Brand-new clothes were in short supply.

_____ c. Only neighborhoods where specks of light showed were bombed.

5. Understanding Main Ideas

One of the statements below expresses the main idea of the passage. One statement is too general, or too broad. The other explains only part of the passage; it is too narrow. Label the statements M for *main idea,* B for *too broad,* and N for *too narrow.*

_____ a. Life in Britain has changed over the ages.

_____ b. People in Great Britain coped with the hardships and changes caused by the Blitz.

_____ c. Food and other goods were rationed during the Blitz.

Correct Answers, Part A _____

Correct Answers, Part B _____

Total Correct Answers _____

Law and Order on the Electronic Frontier

The Internet (Net) is sometimes called the "electronic frontier." Like the Old West, this new frontier offers great opportunities and has few rules; but unlike the Old Western towns, the Internet has no sheriff. There is no public office with the authority or the power to tame it.

As its name suggests, the Internet is a network of computer networks. It is difficult to regulate the Net because it has no central control point. The most popular feature of the Internet is the World Wide Web. When people "surf the Web," they connect to an Internet Service Provider (ISP). Each ISP is part of a regional network that is linked to many larger networks.

At first the Net needed no control. Built in 1969, it was first called the Advanced Research Projects Agency Network (ARPANET). Only scientists working for the Department of Defense used it. The researchers all agreed on two rules: share information and avoid commercial use. By 1992 ARPANET had grown into the World Wide Web. In 1993 the government asked three private companies to manage the network. Businesses and private citizens could now use the Net.

As the Internet grows, lawmakers are not able to keep up. The result is a "policy vacuum." When Manila police arrested the creator of the "Love Bug" virus in 2000, the Philippines had no laws against computer crimes. The virus stole passwords, so police charged the hacker with credit card fraud.

In 2000 France tried to stop Yahoo from selling Nazi items on the Web. Should France's hate-crime law limit what a foreign company can sell on its Web site? There are many other issues to resolve as well. How does the right to privacy apply to e-mail material written at work? May public libraries block access to sites deemed improper for children?

As these issues are being argued, who is keeping order on the new frontier? Users follow their own sense of ethics while ISPs enforce acceptable-use rules. State and national governments pass laws against "cybercrime," scholars propound theories of computer ethics, and computer scientists form groups to promote responsible use of the Net. ICANN, the nonprofit group that manages the Internet, reviews possible reforms.

Despite these valiant efforts, the electronic frontier remains wild. Deceitful people can still entrap the unwary, but taming the Internet poses its own drawbacks by limiting freedom and opportunities on this fast-moving new frontier.

Reading Time _____

Recalling Facts

1. The Internet is best defined as
   - ❑ a. a company of Web sites.
   - ❑ b. the World Wide Web.
   - ❑ c. interconnected computer networks.

2. The Internet was made available for commercial use when
   - ❑ a. private companies began to manage it.
   - ❑ b. the Department of Defense set up ARPANET.
   - ❑ c. an international court ruled that commercial use was legal.

3. Regulating the Internet is difficult because
   - ❑ a. the process is expensive.
   - ❑ b. the Internet has no central control point.
   - ❑ c. only a few governments want to limit access to the Net.

4. The Philippines' lack of laws against computer crimes in 2000 is an example of
   - ❑ a. a cybercriminal.
   - ❑ b. a policy vacuum.
   - ❑ c. an ethical dilemma.

5. Computer ethics is the discipline that involves how to
   - ❑ a. use the Internet responsibly.
   - ❑ b. track computer crimes.
   - ❑ c. stop the spread of computer viruses.

Understanding Ideas

6. The author bases the comparison between the Internet and the Old West on their
   - ❑ a. having a central authority.
   - ❑ b. status as new frontiers.
   - ❑ c. interconnected networks.

7. The experimental network that began the Internet needed few regulations because
   - ❑ a. its users shared no important information.
   - ❑ b. its users were a community that shared the same goals.
   - ❑ c. hackers concentrated on breaking into other networks.

8. France's attempt to regulate Yahoo illustrates
   - ❑ a. a test of the right to freedom of speech.
   - ❑ b. the confusion caused by different network technologies.
   - ❑ c. a conflict in international laws that apply to the Internet.

9. One might conclude from the passage that the future of the Internet will probably be determined by
   - ❑ a. many different groups.
   - ❑ b. the ISPs.
   - ❑ c. the principles behind ARPANET.

10. The author suggests that those trying to make policy for the Internet
    - ❑ a. do so before cybercriminals take over.
    - ❑ b. have few serious issues left to debate.
    - ❑ c. balance freedom and safety.

Virginia Shea: The "Miss Manners" of the Internet

People who write e-mail messages in ALL CAPITAL LETTERS are often accused of having bad "Netiquette." The term, a combination of *network* and *etiquette,* refers to the standards for polite communication on the Internet. Like the word itself, these standards are based on network technology and common courtesy.

When sending e-mail, people see only a computer screen; this makes it easy to ignore the feelings of the person who receives the message. The recipient, too, sees only words on a screen; this means that an angry message can come across more strongly than intended.

Virginia Shea has been called "the 'Miss Manners' of the Internet." Reading columns by Judith Martin, who writes as Miss Manners, shaped Shea's sense of etiquette. Today Shea herself is considered an etiquette expert, and her basic rule is "remember the human." From guidelines posted by various user groups, she learned that using all caps is considered "shouting." She suggests that people say nothing in an e-mail message that they would not say in person. Use emoticons, such as the "smiley-face" symbol, to show feelings. Use acronyms, such as *LOL* (laughing out loud), to help readers understand when a joke is intended. Shea's book *Netiquette,* written in 1994, is considered the first guidebook to proper Internet manners.

1. Recognizing Words in Context

Find the word *standards* in the passage. One definition below is closest to the meaning of that word. One definition has the opposite or nearly the opposite meaning. The remaining definition has a completely different meaning. Label the definitions C for *closest,* O for *opposite or nearly opposite,* and D for *different.*

_____ a. flags

_____ b. exceptions

_____ c. criteria

2. Distinguishing Fact from Opinion

Two of the statements below present *facts,* which can be proved. The other statement is an *opinion,* which expresses someone's thoughts or beliefs. Label the statements F for *fact* and O for *opinion.*

_____ a. Virginia Shea wrote the book *Netiquette.*

_____ b. Virginia Shea has gained a reputation as an expert on Internet etiquette.

_____ c. Virginia Shea's writing is needed more in this electronic age than Judith Martin's.

3. **Keeping Events in Order**

Number the statements below 1, 2, and 3 to show the order in which the events took place.

_____ a. Shea writes *Netiquette*.

_____ b. Shea reads Judith Martin's columns.

_____ c. Shea is recognized as an etiquette expert for communication on the Web.

4. **Making Correct Inferences**

Two of the statements below are correct *inferences*, or reasonable guesses. They are based on information in the passage. The other statement is an incorrect, or faulty, inference. Label the statements C for *correct* inference and F for *faulty* inference.

_____ a. People do not have to worry about politeness on the Internet.

_____ b. Writers should take extra care to avoid having their e-mail messages misinterpreted.

_____ c. Internet etiquette has much in common with everyday etiquette.

5. **Understanding Main Ideas**

One of the statements below expresses the main idea of the passage. One statement is too general, or too broad. The other explains only part of the passage; it is too narrow. Label the statements M for *main idea*, B for *too broad*, and N for *too narrow*.

_____ a. Etiquette sets the standard for good manners.

_____ b. Using all-capital letters in an e-mail message is considered rude.

_____ c. Virginia Shea is an expert on Netiquette.

Correct Answers, Part A _____

Correct Answers, Part B _____

Total Correct Answers _____

8 | A | Pioneers in Women's Rights

In the United States, the nineteenth century was a period of great social reform. The women's rights movement was among these reforms. Its pioneers were drawn in particular from the abolition movement. Two of them, sisters Angelina and Sarah Grimké, were ardent abolitionists. Daughters of slave owners and converts to Quakerism, they were very outspoken. When they spoke in public in 1836 about their own experiences with slavery, they were criticized for stepping beyond the bounds of "proper behavior" for women. This led to their lifelong interest in woman suffrage.

Two other reformers, Lucretia Mott and Elizabeth Cady Stanton, traveled to London in 1840 to attend an international conference on the abolition of slavery. When they arrived, however, they discovered that they would not be allowed to speak and would be forced to sit behind a curtain to watch the proceedings. Such blatant discrimination sparked in these two women the desire to begin their fight for women's rights.

Along with three other women, Mott and Stanton organized a meeting. It was held in Seneca Falls, New York, in 1848 and was attended by 300 people. This meeting became known as the Seneca Falls Convention. Stanton adapted the Declaration of Independence to proclaim that all men *and women* were created equal. Among the rights that women fought for were the right to property ownership, equal rights in a divorce (including custody of their children), and (most controversial) the right to vote. From that point on, Mott and Stanton, along with another Quaker reformer, Susan B. Anthony, campaigned tirelessly for women's rights.

Stanton and Anthony became partners in the fight for women's right to vote. Stanton wrote many of the speeches and pamphlets. Anthony served as organizer and inspirational leader. After the Civil War, when the Fourteenth and Fifteenth amendments gave African American men the rights of citizenship, such as the right to vote, Stanton and Anthony claimed the same rights for women. Anthony and 150 other women voted in the presidential election of 1872 but were later arrested.

Stanton and Anthony continued their fight. Stanton drafted a woman suffrage amendment in 1878. However, it wasn't until 1920 that the Nineteenth Amendment was ratified and women won the right to vote. Neither Stanton nor Anthony lived long enough to see their dream become a reality. The right to vote was just the beginning of the struggle for full equality for women.

Reading Time _____

Recalling Facts

1. The last name of two famous abolitionist sisters was
   - ❑ a. Grimké.
   - ❑ b. Mott.
   - ❑ c. Stanton.

2. The Seneca Falls Convention was held in
   - ❑ a. 1840.
   - ❑ b. 1848.
   - ❑ c. 1920.

3. The woman who drafted a woman suffrage amendment was
   - ❑ a. Lucretia Mott.
   - ❑ b. Elizabeth Cady Stanton.
   - ❑ c. Susan B. Anthony.

4. The constitutional amendment that gave women the right to vote was the
   - ❑ a. Fourteenth.
   - ❑ b. Fifteenth.
   - ❑ c. Nineteenth.

5. The most controversial demand made by people at the Seneca Falls Convention was
   - ❑ a. the right of women to vote.
   - ❑ b. the right of women to own property.
   - ❑ c. equal rights between men and women in a divorce.

Understanding Ideas

6. One can conclude from reading this passage that
   - ❑ a. many Quakers supported reform movements.
   - ❑ b. all abolitionists were Quakers.
   - ❑ c. only Quakers supported women's rights.

7. The event that most directly sparked the organization of the Seneca Falls Convention was the
   - ❑ a. passage of the Fifteenth Amendment.
   - ❑ b. Civil War.
   - ❑ c. abolition conference in London.

8. Susan B. Anthony's experience in 1872 showed that
   - ❑ a. women had won voting rights.
   - ❑ b. women needed a constitutional amendment to gain the right to vote.
   - ❑ c. women and African American men had the same rights.

9. The main idea of this passage is that
   - ❑ a. Lucretia Mott and Elizabeth Cady Stanton attended an international conference on the abolition of slavery.
   - ❑ b. women were satisfied once they had the right to vote.
   - ❑ c. many women fought for a long time to win the right to vote.

10. From the passage, one can infer that
    - ❑ a. all women wanted the right to vote.
    - ❑ b. many men eventually supported woman suffrage.
    - ❑ c. most women opposed woman suffrage.

8   B   Juana Inés de la Cruz, Women's Rights Advocate

Two hundred years before the Seneca Falls Convention of 1848, Juana Inés de la Cruz was born in Mexico. She would become known as Latin America's first women's rights advocate. At that time, Spain was the dominant colonial power in the New World, with a culture in Mexico City rivaling that in European cities.

Born into a wealthy family, Juana Inés de la Cruz was especially influenced by her grandfather. His large library became the basis for her learning. In 1667 Juana entered a convent and continued her studies. Sor (Sister) Juana, as she became known, turned her nun's quarters into a salon where many intellectuals and artists of the day met to exchange ideas.

Sor Juana was a gifted poet and playwright. Her reputation as an early women's rights advocate stems from an essay that she wrote. It was a response to a criticism of her studies by a bishop, who wrote his attack under the pseudonym of a nun. In *Response to Sister Filotea,* written in 1691, Sor Juana expounded movingly on the rights of women to an education and on the benefits society received from educated women. At the time, the essay was the subject of much controversy. Today it is seen as a fine example of resistance to the power exercised over women at that time.

1. **Recognizing Words in Context**

   Find the word *expounded* in the passage. One definition below is closest to the meaning of that word. One definition has the opposite or nearly the opposite meaning. The remaining definition has a completely different meaning. Label the definitions C for *closest*, O for *opposite or nearly opposite*, and D for *different*.

   _____ a. spoke

   _____ b. struck

   _____ c. remained silent

2. **Distinguishing Fact from Opinion**

   Two of the statements below present *facts,* which can be proved. The other statement is an *opinion,* which expresses someone's thoughts or beliefs. Label the statements F for *fact* and O for *opinion.*

   _____ a. Juana Inés de la Cruz was born in Mexico.

   _____ b. Sor Juana was the best writer in Mexico City.

   _____ c. *Response to Sister Filotea* was written in 1691.

3. **Keeping Events in Order**

Number the statements below 1, 2, and 3 to show the order in which the events took place.

_____ a. The Seneca Falls Convention was held.

_____ b. Juana Inés de la Cruz wrote *Response to Sister Filotea*.

_____ c. Juana Inés de la Cruz became a nun.

4. **Making Correct Inferences**

Two of the statements below are correct *inferences*, or reasonable guesses. They are based on information in the passage. The other statement is an incorrect, or faulty, inference. Label the statements C for *correct* inference and F for *faulty* inference.

_____ a. In the seventeenth century, it was unusual for women to be educated.

_____ b. All artists are feminists.

_____ c. Mexico City had a lively creative community in the seventeenth century.

5. **Understanding Main Ideas**

One of the statements below expresses the main idea of the passage. One statement is too general, or too broad. The other explains only part of the passage; it is too narrow. Label the statements M for *main idea*, B for *too broad*, and N for *too narrow*.

_____ a. The women's rights movement was supported in many parts of the world.

_____ b. Poet and playwright Juana Inés de la Cruz was one of the first Latin American advocates of women's rights.

_____ c. Juana Inés de la Cruz met with the leading intellectuals and artists of her day.

Correct Answers, Part A _____

Correct Answers, Part B _____

Total Correct Answers _____

Educating Safe Drivers

In the first years after the invention of the automobile, driving was fairly hazardous. Cars were not well built, and roads were little more than dirt paths. Through the years, however, a number of factors have improved driving safety. Higher-quality car construction, airbags, and restraints such as seatbelts and infant seats all save lives and reduce injuries. Better roads and brighter lighting help prevent accidents. The safest roads, however, are those that have safe drivers on them.

Safe drivers tend to be experienced drivers. Statistics show that new drivers, especially young drivers, are the most likely to become involved in accidents. Although the laws that govern the licensing of drivers vary from state to state, many states have taken steps to improve driver training.

Among the most advanced approaches are intermediate or graduated licensing programs. These programs have three parts. The new driver must be at least 15 years old and enrolled in a driver's education course. New drivers must also pass a written test to obtain a permit that will allow them to practice driving. Some states require that a learner's permit be held for a certain number of months before the license test can be administered. All states require a minimum number of hours of practice with an adult licensed driver in the vehicle. Some states require as few as 12 hours of practice; others mandate as many as 100 hours.

In a graduated licensing program, satisfactory performance on the driving test earns an intermediate license. During the time that new drivers hold an intermediate license, there are severe penalties for moving violations such as speeding or failure to stop at stop signs. There may also be restrictions on driving at night, most commonly between the hours of midnight and 5 A.M. At the end of this probationary period, if the driver has a clean record, he or she receives unrestricted driving privileges.

Such graduated licensing systems are not focused only on teenage drivers. In Maryland, for instance, this approach is called the "rookie driver graduated licensing system." All new drivers, regardless of age, have the same obligations and are measured by the same standards.

It is important to understand that driver's education is not just for the novice driver. Even experienced drivers can benefit from a course designed to improve their skills. A number of courses for mature drivers are available through local driving clubs and other organizations.

Reading Time _____

Recalling Facts

1. Automobile safety is better today because
   - ❏ a. most drivers are more mature than they were in times past.
   - ❏ b. car construction, restraints, and roads have improved.
   - ❏ c. some drivers are experienced and can drive fast.

2. A graduated licensing program
   - ❏ a. allows some novice drivers to avoid a driver's education course.
   - ❏ b. focuses on the needs of mature drivers.
   - ❏ c. has three parts, including a probationary period.

3. The laws that govern the licensing of drivers
   - ❏ a. vary from state to state.
   - ❏ b. are set by federal law.
   - ❏ c. are almost the same in every state.

4. It is common for a driver with an intermediate license
   - ❏ a. to drive with a licensed adult driver in the car.
   - ❏ b. to be a dependable and experienced driver.
   - ❏ c. to be restricted from driving between midnight and 5 A.M.

5. Driver's education
   - ❏ a. is available in only a few states.
   - ❏ b. can benefit experienced as well as novice drivers.
   - ❏ c. does not contribute to roads filled with safer drivers.

Understanding Ideas

6. One can conclude that most states
   - ❏ a. focus on driver's education as a way to make the roads safer.
   - ❏ b. do not offer driver's education courses to experienced drivers.
   - ❏ c. depend on parents to teach their children how to drive.

7. Experienced drivers are better than new drivers at
   - ❏ a. knowing how to avoid getting caught by the police.
   - ❏ b. taking written drivers' exams.
   - ❏ c. avoiding accidents.

8. The idea behind a graduated licensing program may be that
   - ❏ a. teenagers should be kept off the road as much as possible.
   - ❏ b. novice drivers gain more driving privileges as they acquire more experience.
   - ❏ c. police need a way to identify novice drivers.

9. Graduated licensing programs are based on the understanding that
   - ❏ a. new drivers take unacceptable risks.
   - ❏ b. safe drivers are born, not made, but training can be beneficial.
   - ❏ c. safe driving requires complex skills that are best acquired in stages over time.

10. Which of the following best states the main idea of this passage?
   - ❏ a. Driver's education plays an important part in making the roads safer.
   - ❏ b. Road safety is a concern.
   - ❏ c. Graduated licensing systems focus on all new drivers.

9 B   Cell Phones and Driving

New wireless technologies have cut the cord that bound people to telephones in their homes and workplaces and to telephones in stationary telephone booths. The sounds of telephone signals are everywhere—from boulevards and department stores to restaurants and theaters. Many of these conversations are taking place in cars. Anecdotal evidence suggests that talking on the phone while driving causes accidents, but it takes more than a few personal tales to establish a link between cell phones and problems on the road.

Scientists, however, are examining this relationship. One study demonstrates that drivers are more likely to wander from lane to lane and collide with another vehicle when using car phones. Drivers using phones are also more likely to strike pedestrians. "Hands-free" phones appear to be no safer than hand-held phones. Also, using phones in cars appears to be more dangerous for older people than for younger people.

In general, telephones are considered a distraction. Drivers on the phone seem to respond more slowly to changes in traffic or unexpected events. In fact, drivers who talk while they drive are four times as likely to be in an accident as drivers who do not. Drivers using the phone at the time of an accident, moreover, are more likely to suffer a serious or fatal injury than those who focus only on driving.

1. **Recognizing Words in Context**

   Find the word *anecdotal* in the passage. One definition below is closest to the meaning of that word. One definition has the opposite or nearly the opposite meaning. The remaining definition has a completely different meaning. Label the definitions C for *closest,* O for *opposite or nearly opposite,* and D for *different.*

   _____ a. scientifically based

   _____ b. based on informal observation

   _____ c. related to statistics

2. **Distinguishing Fact from Opinion**

   Two of the statements below present *facts,* which can be proved. The other statement is an *opinion,* which expresses someone's thoughts or beliefs. Label the statements F for *fact* and O for *opinion.*

   _____ a. "Hands-free" phones do not appear to be safer than hand-held phones.

   _____ b. People who talk on phones while they drive are slower to respond to changes in traffic.

   _____ c. People should not talk on the phone while driving.

3. Keeping Events in Order

Number the statements below 1, 2, and 3 to show the order in which the events took place.

_____ a. Scientists try to establish a link between cell phones and problems on the road.

_____ b. Drivers make telephone calls in their vehicles.

_____ c. Scientists develop wireless technology.

4. Making Correct Inferences

Two of the statements below are correct *inferences,* or reasonable guesses. They are based on information in the passage. The other statement is an incorrect, or faulty, inference. Label the statements C for *correct* inference and F for *faulty* inference.

_____ a. Cell phones have increased communication but have also created safety problems.

_____ b. Personal experience leads some people to think that drivers' use of cell phones causes accidents.

_____ c. Drivers who talk on cell phones are not paying attention to the road.

5. Understanding Main Ideas

One of the statements below expresses the main idea of the passage. One statement is too general, or too broad. The other explains only part of the passage; it is too narrow. Label the statements M for *main idea,* B for *too broad,* and N for *too narrow.*

_____ a. Drivers are more likely to wander from land to lane when using phones.

_____ b. The popularity of cell phones may be contributing to problems on the roads.

_____ c. Wireless technology has many applications.

Correct Answers, Part A _____

Correct Answers, Part B _____

Total Correct Answers _____

Why Did the Ancient Maya Abandon Their Cities?

The ancient Maya built many large cities in the Classic Period, which lasted from about 250 until about 900. Each city had its own king and ruling class. The cities traded with one another but often fought with one another as well. In about 900, the Maya abandoned many of their cities. Archaeologists and other scientists have long puzzled over why the Maya left. They have formed theories by examining those cities carefully and studying the settlements that surround them. Researchers think that the populations in some places may have grown so large that people abandoned them because there was not enough food for everyone.

Archaeologists studied clues from one city and its surroundings to learn what had happened there. In Copán they found many tools dating from 500 to about 1000 and a few tools dating from about 1000 to 1200. They found that no new monuments had been built after 822. From studying plant remains, scientists concluded that the area around Copán had been farmland. Other evidence suggested that the land was overfarmed. In view of the evidence, the scientists concluded that a large population lived in Copán until about 1000. As more people farmed the land, the soil lost its richness and produced fewer crops, which caused the Maya who lived there to suffer from malnutrition, as analysis of skulls shows. As a result, people began to leave Copán in about 1000, but they did not completely abandon the city until about 1200.

War also may have caused the Maya to abandon some of their cities. For example, it is thought that a rival city, Caracol, may have once conquered Tikal. Then, after more than 100 years had passed, Tikal returned to power, and the ruling family built temples to honor its victory. However, by the end of the 800s, Tikal was no longer powerful. Its inhabitants left the city. Some archaeologists and historians think that war may have broken out again and caused the citizens to leave.

Although we do not know for certain why many ancient Maya abandoned their cities, we may find some clues by observing today's Maya. Modern Maya still live in the lands, including Mexico and Guatemala, that their ancestors occupied. Many present-day Maya practice a variety of ancient beliefs and customs, such as farming practices. Studying their beliefs and practices may help scientists discover more about ancient Mayan culture.

Reading Time _____

Recalling Facts

1. The Maya abandoned many of their cities in about
   - ❑ a. 250.
   - ❑ b. 822.
   - ❑ c. 900.

2. Researchers speculate that some Maya abandoned cities because
   - ❑ a. there was not enough food to eat.
   - ❑ b. there were not enough tools to use.
   - ❑ c. buildings started to crumble.

3. The Maya of Copán did not completely abandon their city until about
   - ❑ a. 800.
   - ❑ b. 1000.
   - ❑ c. 1200.

4. In Copán, scientists found evidence that the Maya had
   - ❑ a. been defeated by the city of Caracol.
   - ❑ b. overfarmed the land and suffered from malnutrition.
   - ❑ c. gone to war.

5. Puzzled about why the ancient Maya left their cities, archaeologists formed theories by
   - ❑ a. examining the cities carefully and studying the surrounding settlements.
   - ❑ b. comparing the Maya to other ancient cultures.
   - ❑ c. studying Mayan legends.

Understanding Ideas

6. It is probable that scientists will not agree on a theory about why the Maya abandoned a particular city
   - ❑ a. until more cities are found.
   - ❑ b. without more physical evidence.
   - ❑ c. until secret modern practices are revealed.

7. One can conclude from the passage that scientists want to know
   - ❑ a. why Tikal was abandoned.
   - ❑ b. who built Tikal.
   - ❑ c. who conquered Tikal.

8. The difference in the number of tools found in Copán between 500 and 1200 suggests that
   - ❑ a. fewer people lived in Copán after 1000 than before 1000.
   - ❑ b. more people lived in Copán after 1000 than before 1000.
   - ❑ c. the number of people living in Copán between 500 and 1200 never changed.

9. If the people of Copán had enriched their soil, it is possible that
   - ❑ a. Copán would still be inhabited.
   - ❑ b. they would have starved.
   - ❑ c. fewer tools would have been found between 500 and 1000.

10. Which of the following statements best describes the main idea?
    - ❑ a. The Classic Period of Mayan civilization lasted from about 250 until about 900.
    - ❑ b. Overfarming was the reason the Maya abandoned Capán.
    - ❑ c. Scientists continue to investigate why the Maya abandoned many of their great cities.

Remnants of the Past

Today one can visit several ancient Mayan city-states (or at least the excavated portions of them). One such city, Tikal, has about 3,000 buildings—such as temples, pyramids, palaces, and houses—many of them still buried. Archaeologists have restored parts of Tikal, including several plazas and buildings linked by broad roads. Royal palaces stand at the center of the city. Beyond them is the North Acropolis, which includes eight temples. Between the palaces and the North Acropolis is a ball court.

In Chichén Itzá, one can also see a ball court, but the Mayan courts look only vaguely similar to today's basketball courts. The court in Chichén Itzá resembles a capital I. Several stone rings, each with a narrow opening in its center, jut out from the stone walls of the ball courts, high above the ground.

Like Tikal, Chichén Itzá has temples, but one can also see several buildings there, including the Caracol Observatory, that the Maya built to watch the skies. After walking up many stairs and going into the round observatory, one walks up a spiral staircase into a small room. The room has windows through which one can watch the Sun, Moon, planets, and stars, about which the Maya kept detailed records.

1. **Recognizing Words in Context**

   Find the word *excavated* in the passage. One definition below is closest to the meaning of that word. One definition has the opposite or nearly the opposite meaning. The remaining definition has a completely different meaning. Label the definitions C for *closest*, O for *opposite or nearly opposite*, and D for *different*.

   _____ a. uncovered

   _____ b. buried

   _____ c. restricted

2. **Distinguishing Fact from Opinion**

   Two of the statements below present *facts*, which can be proved. The other statement is an *opinion*, which expresses someone's thoughts or beliefs. Label the statements F for *fact* and O for *opinion*.

   _____ a. Tikal and Chichén Itzá are two magnificent city-states of the ancient Maya.

   _____ b. Parts of Tikal and Chichén Itzá have been restored.

   _____ c. Both Tikal and Chichén Itzá have ball courts.

3. Keeping Events in Order

Number the statements below 1, 2, and 3 to show the order in which the events took place.

_____ a. One looks at the sky through windows in a small room.

_____ b. One goes into the circular Caracol Observatory.

_____ c. One walks up a spiral staircase.

4. Making Correct Inferences

Two of the statements below are correct *inferences,* or reasonable guesses. They are based on information in the passage. The other statement is an incorrect, or faulty, inference. Label the statements C for *correct* inference and F for *faulty* inference.

_____ a. The game of basketball is a Mayan invention.

_____ b. The Maya were skilled builders.

_____ c. The center of each city-state was reserved for religious purposes and dwellings for the upper classes.

5. Understanding Main Ideas

One of the statements below expresses the main idea of the passage. One statement is too general, or too broad. The other explains only part of the passage; it is too narrow. Label the statements M for *main idea,* B for *too broad,* and N for *too narrow.*

_____ a. Remains of ancient temples, pyramids, palaces, and houses can be seen in many parts of the world.

_____ b. Ball courts and temples were built in Tikal and Chichén Itzá.

_____ c. Evacuated and restored parts of Chichén Itzá and Tikal reveal many details of the ancient Mayan civilization to the visitor.

Correct Answers, Part A _____

Correct Answers, Part B _____

Total Correct Answers _____

Throughout history, people who have relied on agriculture as their way of life have held harvest festivals to celebrate a good growing season. Although fewer people are involved in farming today, the tradition of harvest celebrations continues. People from different backgrounds have adapted practices from other lands.

In some cultures, the harvest festival takes place during the full moon closest to the fall equinox. One such occasion is Tết-Trung-Thu (pronounced *tet-troong-thoo*), which is the Vietnamese Mid-Autumn Festival. The event has become a special holiday for children. Young people receive gifts and candy while they enjoy parades and other forms of entertainment. The Vietnamese continue the tradition of making star lanterns and animal masks.

Another autumn harvest festival is Sukkoth (pronounced *sŏŏ kŏt́* in Hebrew). (Sukkoth comes from *sukka,* meaning "temporary shelter.") The celebration takes place in September or October, the time of harvest in Israel. It commemorates when the Hebrews wandered in the wilderness, living in huts that could easily be moved. Today Jews often build small huts with roofs made of branches. During the eight-day celebration, they may eat, pray, and even sleep in these sukkoth.

Many North American peoples gave thanks for the harvest during the Green Corn festival. The Cherokee usually held their festival in July. Before the celebration, women performed a religious dance. The people built an arch of green branches to cover the grounds, and everyone drank a purifying drink. This festival lasted up to four days. Another famous Native American festival is the Iroquois Strawberry Ceremony, a time of thanksgiving for the strawberry harvest, which usually takes place in May.

The people of Europe also celebrated harvest festivals. In Poland, for example, Dozynski, or Harvest Day, took place about August 15, at the end of the harvest. A village girl wore a crown made of straw. The mayor of the town then put a rooster on top of her crown. As the girl led a procession away from the fields, people listened closely: If the rooster crowed, they believed they would have good luck in the coming year. In another Polish harvest tradition, a female farm worker gave the local noble a wreath made of grain. After he received the gift, the celebration began. Festivals are still held today to honor these traditions.

Reading Time _____

Recalling Facts

1. Harvest festivals were first celebrated by
   - ❏ a. farmers.
   - ❏ b. factory workers.
   - ❏ c. Americans.

2. A harvest festival connected with children is
   - ❏ a. Succoth.
   - ❏ b. Pongal.
   - ❏ c. Têt-Trung-Thu.

3. A harvest festival is held in May by the
   - ❏ a. Jews.
   - ❏ b. Iroquois.
   - ❏ c. Vietnamese.

4. The word for "temporary shelter" is
   - ❏ a. sukka.
   - ❏ b. têt.
   - ❏ c. tabernacle.

5. A rooster was part of the harvest festival in
   - ❏ a. South Asia.
   - ❏ b. Vietnam.
   - ❏ c. Poland.

Understanding Ideas

6. From reading the passage, one can conclude that harvest festivals
   - ❏ a. involve many different rituals.
   - ❏ b. are the same in all cultures.
   - ❏ c. do not occur in the United States.

7. Many harvest festivals are celebrated
   - ❏ a. on alternate years.
   - ❏ b. in the late summer or fall.
   - ❏ c. when a small group of farmers decides to.

8. An element that is common to most of the harvest festivals described in the passage is
   - ❏ a. giving thanks.
   - ❏ b. ritual chanting.
   - ❏ c. flying kites.

9. From reading the passage, one can conclude that
   - ❏ a. crops are harvested at the same time all over the world.
   - ❏ b. different crops are harvested in different months.
   - ❏ c. the timing of harvest festivals always depends on the moon.

10. Harvest festivals
   - ❏ a. are limited to rural farming communities.
   - ❏ b. often incorporate religious traditions.
   - ❏ c. are commercial celebrations.

Was It Really the "First Thanksgiving?"

English settlers arrived at Plymouth, Massachusetts, in December 1620. These Pilgrims had a difficult time surviving their first winter. They had arrived too late to plant crops, and they had not brought with them food sufficient to last until spring.

The native people, called Wampanoag, knew how to plant crops, fish, hunt, and gather foods. They taught the English these skills. Several times each year, the Wampanoag thanked their creator god, Kiehtan, for his bounty, worshipping him in ceremonies that included songs, dances, prayers, and a considerable feast.

The English had their own festivals. The most common was Harvest Home, usually held near the end of September. In this celebration, fruits and vegetables were offered to thank God and to pray for a bountiful crop. Some landowners held a feast at the time of Harvest Home, giving thanks to God and the workers for their hard work.

At their first harvest time in America, the Pilgrims invited the Wampanoag to join them. Undoubtedly, the two cultures shared their traditions. This united festival may not have been the "First Thanksgiving," however. Accounts do not say that it was a feast of thanksgiving, and both the English and the Wampanoag had long celebrated the harvest in their own ways.

1. **Recognizing Words in Context**

    Find the word *sufficient* in the passage. One definition below is closest to the meaning of that word. One definition has the opposite or nearly the opposite meaning. The remaining definition has a completely different meaning. Label the definitions C for *closest*, O for *opposite or nearly opposite*, and D for *different*.

    _____ a. enough

    _____ b. tasty

    _____ c. inadequate

2. **Distinguishing Fact from Opinion**

    Two of the statements below present *facts*, which can be proved. The other statement is an *opinion*, which expresses someone's thoughts or beliefs. Label the statements F for *fact* and O for *opinion*.

    _____ a. The Pilgrims held a harvest festival in 1621.

    _____ b. The Wampanoag taught the English survival skills.

    _____ c. All cultures should celebrate a day of thanksgiving.

3. Keeping Events in Order

Number the statements below 1, 2, and 3 to show the order in which the events took place.

_____ a. The Pilgrims had a harvest festival with the Wampanoag.

_____ b. The Wampanoag helped the Pilgrims learn to farm.

_____ c. The Pilgrims saw that they did not have enough food.

4. Making Correct Inferences

Two of the statements below are correct *inferences,* or reasonable guesses. They are based on information in the passage. The other statement is an incorrect, or faulty, inference. Label the statements C for *correct* inference and F for *faulty* inference.

_____ a. The Wampanoag celebrated harvest festivals before 1621.

_____ b. The Wampanoag gave the Pilgrims the idea for a harvest festival in 1621.

_____ c. Harvest festivals are celebrated in many cultures.

5. Understanding Main Ideas

One of the statements below expresses the main idea of the passage. One statement is too general, or too broad. The other explains only part of the passage; it is too narrow. Label the statements M for *main idea,* B for *too broad,* and N for *too narrow.*

_____ a. The Wampanoag contributed to the Pilgrims' harvest festival in 1621.

_____ b. Giving thanks for the harvest has been a tradition for people in many parts of the world.

_____ c. The harvest festival of 1621 continued traditions held by both the Wampanoag and the English.

Correct Answers, Part A _____

Correct Answers, Part B _____

Total Correct Answers _____

Morocco's long history includes periods of peace, wealth, and strong government as well as times of violence, bankruptcy, and weak leadership. Although Berbers have lived in this northwestern part of Africa for more than 3,000 years, many other peoples have settled there too. The Roman Empire once included parts of Morocco. Other peoples followed the Romans, most staying only a short time. In contrast, the Arabs swept into Morocco in about 680, bringing with them Islam—today the state religion of Morocco. About 100 years later, an Arab ruler united Berbers and Arabs to form the first Moroccan state.

The union did not last, however, and for hundreds of years, a succession of Arab and Berber dynasties ruled in Morocco. Some dynasties ruled empires that stretched across northern Africa and reached into Spain and Portugal. Then, in 1415, Portugal captured one of Morocco's ports. Thereafter Portugal and Spain gained increasing control over coastal Morocco, while the Moroccans battled to drive the Europeans from the country. By the 1800s, France also had become interested in Morocco.

As a result of treaties, military victories, and a bankrupt Moroccan government, France and Spain had gained control over Morocco by the early 1900s. France, and to a lesser extent Spain, kept control for many years. During that time, the French built roads, railroads, and new towns. They reformed the legal system and modernized the government. Settlers from France and Spain governed the country. Moroccans were left with no voice in the government. Dissatisfied and angry, they demanded independence, staging revolts and rioting against foreign control.

Finally, in 1956, Morocco gained its independence. When Hassan II became its king, he adopted the first Moroccan constitution. Hassan II worked to solve many of Morocco's problems, including unemployment and high inflation. He passed laws to increase Moroccan ownership and employment in companies doing business in Morocco. In rural areas, he redistributed foreign-owned farms to Moroccan farmers. He also revised a code of laws to give women more rights. Hassan II did not solve all of Morocco's problems during his lifetime, but many experts agree that he left the country in better condition than it had been in when he came to power. Today his son, Mohammed VI, is furthering his goals. Mohammed VI has also made education for all Moroccan children a priority, in part because he considers education the basis for progress.

Reading Time _____

Recalling Facts

1. Berbers have lived in Morocco
   - ❑ a. for more than 3,000 years.
   - ❑ b. since 680.
   - ❑ c. for about 100 years.

2. Some Moroccan empires reached into
   - ❑ a. France and Spain.
   - ❑ b. France and Portugal.
   - ❑ c. Spain and Portugal.

3. France and Spain gained control over Morocco as a result of
   - ❑ a. an outdated government and the lack of roads.
   - ❑ b. various treaties, military victories, and a bankrupt Moroccan government.
   - ❑ c. revolts and riots in Morocco.

4. Morocco gained its independence in
   - ❑ a. 680.
   - ❑ b. the 1800s.
   - ❑ c. 1956.

5. One of Mohammed VI's priorities is
   - ❑ a. gaining independence from France.
   - ❑ b. education for all Moroccan children.
   - ❑ c. granting farmland to Moroccan farmers.

Understanding Ideas

6. One can conclude from the passage that
   - ❑ a. Morocco, Spain, and Portugal became trade partners.
   - ❑ b. Moroccan control over Spain and Portugal did not last.
   - ❑ c. Portugal eventually controlled Morocco.

7. The European country that has probably influenced Morocco most is
   - ❑ a. Portugal.
   - ❑ b. Spain.
   - ❑ c. France.

8. It is likely that Hassan II was a
   - ❑ a. strong ruler.
   - ❑ b. weak ruler.
   - ❑ c. violent ruler.

9. One can infer from the passage that Mohammed VI is most interested in
   - ❑ a. personal gain.
   - ❑ b. keeping things as they are.
   - ❑ c. improving the lives of all Moroccans.

10. It appears that economic and social changes in Morocco
    - ❑ a. will not happen, even over long periods of time.
    - ❑ b. will occur slowly but surely.
    - ❑ c. will take only a brief time to establish.

The Journeys of Ibn Battuta

Born in Morocco, Ibn Battuta was a traveler and writer who lived from 1304 to about 1370. At that time, travel was difficult and often unsafe. Disease, shipwrecks, and attacks by robbers were common perils. Ibn Battuta traveled about 75,000 miles during his lifetime. He visited the lands of every Muslim ruler and a few other places as well, journeying to places that today are 44 countries.

Ibn Battuta's travels began when he made his first pilgrimage to Mecca. According to Islam, all Muslims who can make a trip to Mecca must do so. In 1325, Ibn Battuta decided to make his. During the trip, which lasted about a year and a half, he studied with teachers and judges.

After his pilgrimage, he continued to travel, visiting places in Africa, Asia, and Europe. Finally he went to India, where he became a judge. After several years in India, Ibn Battuta resumed his visits to other countries, including China. In the late 1340s, he returned to Morocco after more than 20 years.

After two more expeditions, Ibn Battuta returned to Morocco permanently. He told his stories to its ruler, the sultan. At the sultan's request, he dictated his adventures to a famous literary figure who refined Ibn Battuta's simple prose style. Today the book provides a detailed account of life in the 1300s.

1. **Recognizing Words in Context**

   Find the word *perils* in the passage. One definition below is closest to the meaning of that word. One definition has the opposite or nearly the opposite meaning. The remaining definition has a completely different meaning. Label the definitions C for *closest*, O for *opposite or nearly opposite*, and D for *different*.

   _____ a. accidents

   _____ b. safeguards

   _____ c. dangers

2. **Distinguishing Fact from Opinion**

   Two of the statements below present *facts*, which can be proved. The other statement is an *opinion*, which expresses someone's thoughts or beliefs. Label the statements F for *fact* and O for *opinion*.

   _____ a. Ibn Battuta's adventures were more exciting than those of anyone else.

   _____ b. Ibn Battuta's first trip to Mecca took about a year and a half.

   _____ c. Ibn Battuta spent several years in India.

3. Keeping Events in Order

Number the statements below 1, 2, and 3 to show the order in which the events took place.

_____ a. Ibn Battuta made his first pilgrimage to Mecca.

_____ b. Ibn Battuta dictated his travels at the sultan's request.

_____ c. Ibn Battuta traveled to India.

4. Making Correct Inferences

Two of the statements below are correct *inferences,* or reasonable guesses. They are based on information in the passage. The other statement is an incorrect, or faulty, inference. Label the statements C for *correct* inference and F for *faulty* inference.

_____ a. Ibn Battuta enjoyed travel.

_____ b. Ibn Battuta was curious.

_____ c. Ibn Battuta traveled because he didn't like Morocco.

5. Understanding Main Ideas

One of the statements below expresses the main idea of the passage. One statement is too general, or too broad. The other explains only part of the passage; it is too narrow. Label the statements M for *main idea,* B for *too broad,* and N for *too narrow.*

_____ a. Ibn Battuta traveled throughout the Muslim world in the fourteenth century and wrote a historically important account of life at that time.

_____ b. Travelers in the fourteenth century faced perils such as disease, shipwrecks, and attacks by robbers.

_____ c. Ibn Battuta's travels began in 1325, when he started his first pilgrimage to Mecca.

Correct Answers, Part A _____

Correct Answers, Part B _____

Total Correct Answers _____

"Reading" Textiles to Reveal the Past

Technicians on the popular television show *CSI: Crime Scene Investigation* solve murders by analyzing every scrap of evidence. They may examine a thread found on a victim's body under a microscope. Learning the source of the fiber may help them find the killer. Archaeologists also analyze fibers, remains, and other evidence, but the mysteries that they try to solve are thousands of years old.

One such mystery was why fibers from mummified alpacas found at El Yaral, Peru, are so much softer than those from modern animals. Under a projection microscope, the fibers measured 17.9 micrometers, almost as fine as cashmere, yet fibers from modern alpacas and llamas are so coarse that they are used only in blankets. The discovery of the 1,000-year-old mummies at El Yaral sparked a program to restore the purebred lines created by the Incas. Because cashmere sells for $70 a pound, restoring the fine-fiber breeds could boost Peru's economy.

Even scraps of cloth can reveal how people of ancient cultures lived and worked. Irene Good, a textile archaeologist, has developed new ways of working with ancient textiles. She reads ancient garments by counting threads and re-creating the methods used to produce them. The weavers of ancient Peru were so skilled that one piece of fabric might reveal several techniques. Their work was prized, so it was passed down from generation to generation. Good has almost 5,000 complete pieces to study.

Darrell Gudrum reads ancient textiles by interpreting their designs. One mantle, or cloak, from ancient Peru had more than 120 symbols on it. The cloak showed many constellations, so Gudrum compared them with those on the Inca calendar. He concluded that the cloak was a "farmer's almanac," showing when to plant and harvest crops. The mantle also had symbols related to religious rituals.

Another way to learn about the past is to study living weavers. Women in Peru still use techniques passed down through oral tradition. Nilda Callañaupa founded the Center for Traditional Textiles of Cusco to preserve this heritage. She has already found a village where weavers use a rare technique thought to be extinct. The center documents the methods and symbols used by weavers in remote villages such as Pitumarca. It also creates opportunities for young women to learn these traditions. The textile collection will help people in Peru and around the world learn to read the past from pieces of cloth.

Reading Time _____

Recalling Facts

1. Textile archaeologists are experts in
   - ❏ a. animal mummies.
   - ❏ b. ancient fabrics.
   - ❏ c. solving crimes.

2. One method used by textile archaeologists is to
   - ❏ a. analyze all types of remains.
   - ❏ b. study mummification techniques.
   - ❏ c. examine fibers with a projection microscope.

3. Irene Good is recognized for studying ancient textiles by relying on
   - ❏ a. DNA analysis.
   - ❏ b. thread counting.
   - ❏ c. oral tradition.

4. After studying a cloak from ancient Peru, Darrell Goodrum concluded that the cloak could be compared with
   - ❏ a. an almanac.
   - ❏ b. a weapon carrier.
   - ❏ c. a religious ritual.

5. In Peru ancient weaving traditions have been preserved
   - ❏ a. by many textile museums.
   - ❏ b. through government orders.
   - ❏ c. through oral tradition.

Understanding Ideas

6. From a comparison of ancient and modern alpaca fibers, one can conclude that
   - ❏ a. the Incas had secret methods for treating Alpaca fibers.
   - ❏ b. ancient and modern Alpaca breeds have differences.
   - ❏ c. ancient Alpacas lived longer than their modern counterparts.

7. One can infer that the techniques used by textile archaeologists are
   - ❏ a. among the oldest.
   - ❏ b. too new to be trustworthy.
   - ❏ c. still developing as this new field grows.

8. One sign that textiles were important to ancient Peruvians is the number of
   - ❏ a. pieces that survived.
   - ❏ b. symbols on an ancient cloak.
   - ❏ c. techniques used in one piece.

9. Darrell Gudrum's work with an ancient cloak shows that textile archaeologists
   - ❏ a. are experts in ancient farming technology.
   - ❏ b. use their knowledge of ancient culture to interpret symbols.
   - ❏ c. cannot rely on living weavers to help them.

10. Which statement best sums up the passage?
   - ❏ a. Textile archaeologists study ancient fibers.
   - ❏ b. Textile archaeologists can "read" the past if complete garments are discovered.
   - ❏ c. Textile archaeologists have developed techniques to study evidence in ancient textiles.

Elizabeth Barber, Textile Archaeologist

Pots and spear points can survive for centuries. Fabric is so fragile that, in the past, archaeologists sometimes did not even try to preserve it. Now experts such as Elizabeth Wayland Barber are showing that textiles can reveal information about the past.

Barber is a leader in the new field of textile archaeology. One of her special interests is prehistoric cloth and clothing. For 13 years, she worked mostly with pieces of old cloth smaller than her thumbnail. Her interests are reflected in the titles of two early works: *Prehistoric Textiles,* published in 1991, and *Women's Work,* published in 1994.

In 1995 Barber was one of three Western scholars invited to view the Cherchen mummies. These mummies, found in a desert area of China, are at least 3,000 years old. The hot, dry desert preserved their skin and the clothing that had been buried with them.

One pattern in the fabrics found with the mummies was much like Celtic tartans. Could these Caucasian-looking mummies have migrated to China from Europe? Barber confirmed that the fibers and weaving techniques in the fabrics originated in Europe. She also used linguistic clues to trace the nomads' journey to Asia. Her book on the subject, *The Mummies of Ürümchi,* was published in 1999.

1. **Recognizing Words in Context**
   Find the word *originated* in the passage. One definition below is closest to the meaning of that word. One definition has the opposite or nearly the opposite meaning. The remaining definition has a completely different meaning. Label the definitions C for *closest,* O for *opposite or nearly opposite,* and D for *different.*

   _____ a. started

   _____ b. ended

   _____ c. followed

2. **Distinguishing Fact from Opinion**
   Two of the statements below present *facts,* which can be proved. The other statement is an *opinion,* which expresses someone's thoughts or beliefs. Label the statements F for *fact* and O for *opinion.*

   _____ a. Mummies were found in western China.

   _____ b. Cloth was buried with them.

   _____ c. One design in the fabric was particularly beautiful.

3. Keeping Events in Order

Number the statements below 1, 2, and 3 to show the order in which the events took place.

_____ a. Elizabeth Barber studied tiny scraps of prehistoric fabric.

_____ b. Elizabeth Barber went to China.

_____ c. Elizabeth Barber wrote *The Mummies of Ürümchi.*

4. Making Correct Inferences

Two of the statements below are correct *inferences,* or reasonable guesses. They are based on information in the passage. The other statement is an incorrect, or faulty, inference. Label the statements C for *correct* inference and F for *faulty* inference.

_____ a. Many scholars disagree with Barber's theories about the mummies.

_____ b. Archaeologists are learning new ways to analyze ancient textiles.

_____ c. The clothing buried with the mummies of Ürümchi is a rare find.

5. Understanding Main Ideas

One of the statements below expresses the main idea of the passage. One statement is too general, or too broad. The other explains only part of the passage; it is too narrow. Label the statements M for *main idea,* B for *too broad,* and N for *too narrow.*

_____ a. Barber wrote books about her research in textile archaeology.

_____ b. Archaeologists are capable of providing critical information about earlier times.

_____ c. Barber's work is developing a new field, textile archaeology.

Correct Answers, Part A _____

Correct Answers, Part B _____

Total Correct Answers _____

A person seeking a new career opportunity might consider looking in a museum. Museums provide jobs in fields such as research, management, graphic arts, public relations, education, preserving, cataloging, fund-raising, and construction. A museum may have one employee or thousands.

Many museum workers do not work directly with the objects in the museum; for example, the staff of a finance department prepares budgets and financial reports. Accountant and bookkeeper are typical positions. Staffers in the development department, meanwhile, work to increase museum membership and donations and to plan fund-raisers, such as dances or auctions. Publications department personnel may write newsletters, brochures, or books.

Some museums have an education department responsible for planning talks, teaching workshops, directing tours, or training tour guides.

People who prefer to work directly with a museum's collection have many career options. A person who pays attention to detail may enjoy being a registrar, the person who keeps track of the objects in a museum. Registrars keep records of objects, noting what they are, when and how they were obtained, and whether they are on loan to another museum or on display.

Curators are the people responsible for a museum's collection. One of their duties is to choose items for exhibits; then they work closely with designers who plan the best way to arrange exhibits. Other specialists do things such as arrange lighting or build display cases. Expert craftspeople can also find jobs re-creating historic buildings, such as the Pilgrim village at Plimoth Plantation.

A museum also often employs conservators to repair and take care of its collection. Many conservators are specialists who care for one kind of item, such as books or paintings. The Henry Ford Museum employs many conservators, including some who are experts in caring for antique cars.

Some historic homes, such as George Washington's home in Mount Vernon, have gardens, farms, and woods, as well as buildings. Gardeners are employed to care for the grounds and livestock handlers to care for farm animals.

Museums offer many other career opportunities too. They may have gift shops where sales assistants sell books, postcards, and other items or restaurants where meals are prepared and served. Depending on one's interests, a museum could be a great place to look for a job.

Reading Time _____

Recalling Facts

1. A development department's employees
   - ❏ a. give tours.
   - ❏ b. plan fund-raisers.
   - ❏ c. keep records.

2. A museum's education department might
   - ❏ a. conduct workshops.
   - ❏ b. prepare financial reports.
   - ❏ c. write brochures.

3. Curators are responsible for
   - ❏ a. repairing books and paintings.
   - ❏ b. keeping museum records.
   - ❏ c. maintaining museum collections.

4. Conservators perform such tasks as
   - ❏ a. choosing items for exhibits.
   - ❏ b. preparing and monitoring budgets.
   - ❏ c. repairing and caring for objects in the collections.

5. A person who wants to work directly with a museum collection may become a
   - ❏ a. registrar.
   - ❏ b. bookkeeper.
   - ❏ c. fund-raiser.

Understanding Ideas

6. One can infer from the passage that a publications department in a museum employs
   - ❏ a. writers.
   - ❏ b. teachers.
   - ❏ c. craftspeople.

7. A career as an educator in an art museum would probably require a background in
   - ❏ a. finance.
   - ❏ b. art history.
   - ❏ c. public speaking.

8. Like curators, conservators
   - ❏ a. work directly with museum collections.
   - ❏ b. repair museum collections.
   - ❏ c. prepare financial reports.

9. One can infer from the passage that the Henry Ford Museum probably has a collection of
   - ❏ a. old games.
   - ❏ b. antique cars.
   - ❏ c. dolls.

10. Which of the following statements best describes the main idea of the passage?
    - ❏ a. Curators work closely with designers in the arrangement of museum exhibits.
    - ❏ b. There are many kinds of museums in such fields as history, art, and science.
    - ❏ c. Museums, although they vary in purpose and size, offer a wide range of career opportunities.

Yvonne loved visiting museums and looking at the exhibits. She wanted to work in a museum after she graduated from college, so she consulted museum Web sites on the Internet to find out about the kinds of skills she would need. She soon learned that by volunteering at a museum she could gain experience and learn how a museum operates.

Yvonne searched the Web for a nearby museum and was pleased to see that the museum had many volunteer opportunities. She read that she could water plants in the greenhouses or answer phones in an office. She could volunteer at the information desk, greeting visitors and giving them directions. She could volunteer in the public relations department, assembling press packets. Then she saw a volunteer position that fit her interests perfectly. She could work as a docent, giving tours to visitors and telling them about the museum's collection.

Without hesitation Yvonne called the museum and asked how to become a docent. She learned that she would first have to complete an application and arrange for an interview. If accepted as a docent, she would then take classes for eight months to learn about the museum's collection. After that she would be ready to give her first tour. Flushed with excitement, Yvonne requested an application. Already she could picture herself giving her first tour.

1. **Recognizing Words in Context**

   Find the word *docent* in the passage. One definition below is closest to the meaning of that word. One definition has the opposite or nearly the opposite meaning. The remaining definition has a completely different meaning. Label the definitions C for *closest*, O for *opposite or nearly opposite*, and D for *different*.

   _____ a. viewer

   _____ b. guide

   _____ c. director

2. **Distinguishing Fact from Opinion**

   Two of the statements below present *facts*, which can be proved. The other statement is an *opinion*, which expresses someone's thoughts or beliefs. Label the statements F for *fact* and O for *opinion*.

   _____ a. One can volunteer at a museum to gain experience.

   _____ b. Volunteering at a museum is the best way to learn how a museum operates.

   _____ c. Some museums have a wide range of volunteer opportunities.

3. Keeping Events in Order

Number the statements below 1, 2, and 3 to show the order in which the events took place.

_____ a. Yvonne graduates from college.

_____ b. Yvonne learns about volunteering as a docent.

_____ c. Yvonne plans to work in a museum.

4. Making Correct Inferences

Two of the statements below are correct *inferences,* or reasonable guesses. They are based on information in the passage. The other statement is an incorrect, or faulty, inference. Label the statements C for *correct* inference and F for *faulty* inference.

_____ a. People who volunteer at museums usually enjoy visiting museums.

_____ b. Mostly college students volunteer at museums.

_____ c. Becoming a docent at a museum requires knowing about the content of the museum.

5. Understanding Main Ideas

One of the statements below expresses the main idea of the passage. One statement is too general, or too broad. The other explains only part of the passage; it is too narrow. Label the statements M for *main idea,* B for *too broad,* and N for *too narrow.*

_____ a. After learning about volunteer positions at a museum, Yvonne chose one that suited her.

_____ b. Volunteering at a museum is a type of community service.

_____ c. One can water plants or answer phones as a volunteer at a museum.

Correct Answers, Part A _____

Correct Answers, Part B _____

Total Correct Answers _____

15　A　　The Russian Revolution of 1917

In order to understand why the Russian Revolution of 1917 occurred, one must first understand what life was like in the Russian Empire in pre-Revolutionary days. For hundreds of years, czars, or emperors, ruled Russia. The czar and other wealthy landowners represented only 20 percent of the population. Most of the people were poor peasants and workers, who lived in crowded conditions and could neither read nor write. These people had virtually no say in their government. The czar's rule was absolute, and his advisors wanted no changes in the system. Although an elected parliament (Duma) existed, most of its members were wealthy landowners. The czar could dismiss it anytime he wanted and then demand the election of a new one. Over the years, the people became resentful of the czar's nearly complete control over their country and their lives. Many longed for improved working conditions or more land. Others wished for changes in the structure of the government.

World War I added to the hardships. By 1917 Russia had been at war for nearly three years. People were suffering from shortages of food and fuel, among other supplies. Many educated people believed that the czar's decisions, such as appointing weak government officials and leaving the capital to command the armed forces, had doomed the war effort.

In March 1917, shortages of bread and coal caused the Russian people to revolt. Instead of subduing the rioters, Russian soldiers joined them. With the czar away fighting, parliament appointed a temporary government. A committee of soldiers and workers soon assumed control.

The czar surrendered to the revolutionaries. In the ensuing months, they organized their forces, setting up a number of councils called *soviets*. Members were workers, peasants, soldiers, and others. Vladimir Ilich Lenin, a revolutionary leader who believed in communism, urged the soviets to seize the power of the temporary government. He promised peace, land for the peasants, and factories controlled by the workers. World War I, strikes, and other crises plagued the temporary government.

Finally, Lenin thought that the time was right to seize power. Early in November, the well-organized revolutionaries stormed the temporary government's headquarters, arrested its members, and took control of Russia. Although Lenin and his followers seized power quickly, they then had to fight a civil war and control peasant uprisings and workers' strikes in order to hold onto and build their power.

Reading Time _____

Recalling Facts

1. Most people in pre-Revolutionary Russia were
   - ❑ a. middle class merchants.
   - ❑ b. soldiers.
   - ❑ c. poor peasants and workers.

2. In pre-Revolutionary Russia, peasants and workers
   - ❑ a. elected the czar.
   - ❑ b. held almost no power in the government.
   - ❑ c. were content because they were cared for.

3. Shortages of bread and coal caused
   - ❑ a. Russia to fight World War I.
   - ❑ b. soldiers to hand out food.
   - ❑ c. Russians to revolt.

4. Lenin urged the soviets to
   - ❑ a. take power.
   - ❑ b. cooperate with the temporary government.
   - ❑ c. hold an election.

5. Lenin promised
   - ❑ a. peace, land for the peasants, and factories controlled by the workers.
   - ❑ b. to win World War I.
   - ❑ c. to put an end to strikes.

Understanding Ideas

6. One can infer from the passage that the czar
   - ❑ a. tried to meet the needs of peasants and workers.
   - ❑ b. was an excellent leader.
   - ❑ c. was unable to meet the needs of most Russians.

7. It is likely that the temporary government
   - ❑ a. met the needs of the people.
   - ❑ b. operated ineffectively.
   - ❑ c. was supported by the peasants and workers.

8. One can infer from the passage that the peasants
   - ❑ a. wanted to work in factories.
   - ❑ b. did not have enough land.
   - ❑ c. remained loyal to the czar.

9. If people had been satisfied with their lives, it is likely that
   - ❑ a. a revolution would not have occurred.
   - ❑ b. a revolution would have taken place sooner.
   - ❑ c. World War I would not have occurred.

10. Lenin probably thought that the time was right to seize power because
   - ❑ a. the czar was planning to regain his power.
   - ❑ b. the temporary government was beginning to gain the support of the masses.
   - ❑ c. political and economic instability permitted a government takeover.

The Theory of Communism

The word *communism* comes from a Latin word meaning "common" or "belonging to all." Many people have supported communist ideals such as equality of work and shared profit. In the 1800s, Karl Marx and Friedrich Engels turned the concept of communism into a theory of revolution.

Marx and Engels were aware of the poor pay, long hours, and dangerous working conditions of European factory workers. Both men believed that the workers' situation would not change without a struggle. The men reasoned that a minority of people owned or controlled the means of production, such as land, factories, and money. Most people were workers who controlled nothing except their ability to work. The ruling class kept most of the profits from the goods produced. Marx and Engels argued that the ruling class would not give up its power and profits freely. Therefore, they said, workers must take them. Marx and Engels thought that, with workers controlling the government, society change so that all people would live in peace and be equal and prosperous.

Vladimir Ilich Lenin believed in communism, but he thought that the workers needed a group of dedicated revolutionaries to lead them. In 1917 in Russia, Lenin put his theory of communism into practice. He led into revolt people who believed in a classless society in which all would live well.

1. **Recognizing Words in Context**

   Find the word *minority* in the passage. One definition below is closest to the meaning of that word. One definition has the opposite or nearly the opposite meaning. The remaining definition has a completely different meaning. Label the definitions C for *closest,* O for *opposite or nearly opposite,* and D for *different.*

   _____ a. the smaller of two groups

   _____ b. the majority

   _____ c. a collection

2. **Distinguishing Fact from Opinion**

   Two of the statements below present *facts,* which can be proved. The other statement is an *opinion,* which expresses someone's thoughts or beliefs. Label the statements F for *fact* and O for *opinion.*

   _____ a. After workers controlled the government, society would change so that all people would be equal.

   _____ b. Marx and Engels developed a theory of revolution.

   _____ c. Lenin believed in communism.

3. Keeping Events in Order

Number the statements below 1, 2, and 3 to show the order in which the events took place.

_____ a. In European factories, workers endured low wages, long hours, and dangerous conditions.

_____ b. Marx and Engels developed the concept of communist revolution.

_____ c. Lenin believed that dedicated revolutionaries should lead the people.

4. Making Correct Inferences

Two of the statements below are correct *inferences,* or reasonable guesses. They are based on information in the passage. The other statement is an incorrect, or faulty, inference. Label the statements C for *correct* inference and F for *faulty* inference.

_____ a. Marx and Engels proved that the theory of communism worked.

_____ b. Marx and Engels believed that the ruling class took advantage of the workers.

_____ c. Communism probably appealed to few factory owners.

5. Understanding Main Ideas

One of the statements below expresses the main idea of the passage. One statement is too general, or too broad. The other explains only part of the passage; it is too narrow. Label the statements M for *main idea,* B for *too broad,* and N for *too narrow.*

_____ a. Marx and Engels believed that society would be better if workers were in control.

_____ b. Marx and Engels developed a communist theory of revolution that Lenin adapted.

_____ c. Many people support ideals such as equality of work and shared profits.

Correct Answers, Part A _____

Correct Answers, Part B _____

Total Correct Answers _____

Hands-off Policies of Calvin Coolidge

Calvin Coolidge was president of the United States from 1923 to 1929. His policies made him popular with the public and big business, two groups that wanted less government control of their affairs. During his presidency, Coolidge approved plans to cut government spending and reduce federal taxes, including those for business. His secretary of the treasury, Andrew W. Mellon, thought that big business would profit more if it paid less in taxes. He believed that the profit would help the nation as a whole. At first, the tax cuts did encourage business to increase the production of goods, such as cars and radios. However, businesses eventually produced more goods than people could afford to buy.

While in office, Coolidge vetoed many bills that would have regulated business. Like many Americans of his time, he believed that state and local governments should regulate business and that the federal government should step in only when absolutely necessary.

Coolidge did, however, think that the federal government should promote business interests at home and abroad, and he approved federal spending when it would build a base for business. He supported tariffs, or taxes, on foreign-made goods to protect American manufacturing. As a result, Americans bought American-made goods because they were cheaper than goods made in foreign countries.

Although he was willing to develop a sound base for business, Coolidge opposed government efforts to help business directly. During the 1920s, the price of farm goods fell because of a surplus of crops. Many farmers went into debt and lost their land. Coolidge, however, vetoed farm-aid bills that would have allowed the government to buy surplus crops. He also opposed a bill to aid flood victims. Private business interests such as contractors, he thought, would get most of the aid.

Believing that business would take care of itself, Coolidge set up the Division of Trade Practice Conference within the Federal Trade Commission. The division organized business conferences at which members of a particular industry reached agreements about what defined fair-trade practices within their industry. The agreements effectively blocked individuals and companies from bringing lawsuits claiming that companies were engaging in unfair trade practices.

Although American spending had increased by the time Coolidge left office, economic prosperity was to crumble before the end of the 1920s.

Reading Time _____

Recalling Facts

1. During Coolidge's presidency, both the public and big business wanted
   - ❑ a. more government control of their affairs.
   - ❑ b. less government control of their affairs.
   - ❑ c. the government's role to remain unchanged.

2. Coolidge reduced federal taxes for big business because
   - ❑ a. he thought that this would benefit both big business and the whole nation.
   - ❑ b. then he could tax citizens more.
   - ❑ c. he thought that business produced too many goods.

3. Coolidge supported tariffs on foreign-made goods to
   - ❑ a. encourage foreign trade.
   - ❑ b. protect American manufacturing.
   - ❑ c. make it easier for Americans to buy foreign goods.

4. Coolidge approved federal spending when it would
   - ❑ a. help farmers.
   - ❑ b. build a base for business.
   - ❑ c. help business directly.

5. Coolidge set up the Division of Trade Practice Conference because he believed that
   - ❑ a. it was a good way to attract foreign business to the United States.
   - ❑ b. government spending needed to be cut.
   - ❑ c. business would take care of itself.

Understanding Ideas

6. One can conclude from the passage that Coolidge's policies
   - ❑ a. increased sales of foreign goods in the United States.
   - ❑ b. decreased consumer buying.
   - ❑ c. were effective in the short term but not in the long run.

7. One way that Coolidge demonstrated a hands-off approach to business was by
   - ❑ a. cutting government spending.
   - ❑ b. proposing funding for the airline industry.
   - ❑ c. setting up the Division of Trade Practice Conference.

8. Coolidge helped business by
   - ❑ a. opposing a bill to aid flood victims.
   - ❑ b. supporting high tariffs for foreign-made goods.
   - ❑ c. encouraging competition between foreign-made and American-made goods.

9. One can conclude that big business
   - ❑ a. controlled the Division of Trade Practice Conference.
   - ❑ b. was restricted by the Division of Trade Practice Conference.
   - ❑ c. had very little power during the Coolidge administration.

10. Without Coolidge's hands-off policies, it is possible that
    - ❑ a. production of goods and consumer spending would have increased more slowly.
    - ❑ b. state governments would have regulated business more closely.
    - ❑ c. farmers would not have gone into debt and lost their land.

As the 1920s progressed, American businesses were thriving and the economy booming. Many people were investing money in the stock market and buying shares of stock.

Between 1925 and 1929, the value of most stocks more than doubled. Investors who sold their shares when the price increased made a great deal of money. This led numerous speculators to borrow money to invest in the stock market. They planned to sell their shares when the stock increased in value. However, this injection of money into the market inflated stock prices beyond the worth of the stocks. On October 24, 1929, the surge in stock prices turned into a plunge. By October 29, stock prices had decreased even further, causing numerous investors to panic and sell their stocks, even though the stocks were worth less than their purchase price.

By the end of the year, investors had lost billions in the stock market crash. Banks and businesses that had lost heavily in the stock market closed. Millions of people lost their savings when banks failed. As banks and businesses closed, the people they employed lost their jobs. The stock market crash of 1929 contributed to the decline of the American economy and the resulting Great Depression, which would last into the 1940s in the United States.

1. **Recognizing Words in Context**

   Find the word *surge* in the passage. One definition below is closest to the meaning of that word. One definition has the opposite or nearly the opposite meaning. The remaining definition has a completely different meaning. Label the definitions C for *closest,* O for *opposite or nearly opposite,* and D for *different.*

   _____ a. decline

   _____ b. increase

   _____ c. divide

2. **Distinguishing Fact from Opinion**

   Two of the statements below present *facts,* which can be proved. The other statement is an *opinion,* which expresses someone's thoughts or beliefs. Label the statements F for *fact* and O for *opinion.*

   _____ a. By the end of 1929, investors had lost billions in the stock market crash.

   _____ b. Panicky investors sold their stocks.

   _____ c. The stock market crash was the worst crisis the United States had experienced.

3. Keeping Events in Order

Number the statements below 1, 2, and 3 to show the order in which the events took place.

_____ a. The surge in stock prices turned into a plunge.

_____ b. Many investors lost billions in the stock market crash.

_____ c. Many speculators borrowed money to invest in the stock market.

4. Making Correct Inferences

Two of the statements below are correct *inferences,* or reasonable guesses. They are based on information in the passage. The other statement is an incorrect, or faulty, inference. Label the statements C for *correct* inference and F for *faulty* inference.

_____ a. The stock market might have recovered if investors had not panicked and sold their stock.

_____ b. The American economy was not as strong as it had appeared before the stock market crash.

_____ c. Borrowing money weakens the economy.

5. Understanding Main Ideas

One of the statements below expresses the main idea of the passage. One statement is too general, or too broad. The other explains only part of the passage; it is too narrow. Label the statements M for *main idea,* B for *too broad,* and N for *too narrow.*

_____ a. People panicked when the stock market crashed.

_____ b. President Coolidge's hands-off policy affected the American economy.

_____ c. Speculation and panic caused the stock market to crash, weakening the economy.

Correct Answers, Part A _____

Correct Answers, Part B _____

Total Correct Answers _____

The Santa Fe Trail and the Opening of the Southwest

In the early years of the nineteenth century, the United States extended only as far west as the border between Kansas and Missouri. At that time, most of what is now Texas, New Mexico, Arizona, and southern California was part of Mexico. Mexico was ruled by Spain, a country that was hostile to trade between its Mexican provinces and the United States. As a result, travel between the United States and the Southwest was limited. Mexico's independence from Spain in 1821 opened up opportunities for daring and innovative traders and for eventual U.S. settlement of the Southwest.

In contrast to Spanish policy, the Mexican government was open to trade with the United States. Aware of the money to be made, William Becknell, a Missouri trader, transported a load of goods from western Missouri to Santa Fe, New Mexico, in 1821. His route followed an old trail long used by Native Americans, fur trappers, and explorers. It meandered westward along the Arkansas River and then turned southward through the mountains. At Santa Fe, Becknell found a population long deprived of supplies and manufactured goods. His merchandise fetched high prices.

Becknell planned a second trip. This time, instead of pack horses, he used mule-drawn wagons. He also decided to follow a shorter route, which turned south some 150 miles east of La Junta, Colorado. This route, however, crossed an expanse of desert. Becknell and his party nearly died of thirst before they found the Cimarron River. This new route sliced 10 days from the trip. Soon 75 percent of the traffic between Missouri and Santa Fe used this route. Becknell's route became known as the Santa Fe Trail. His pioneering journeys opened Santa Fe for trade and earned him the nickname Father of the Santa Fe Trail.

Word of the eager buyers in Santa Fe spread quickly. Within a few years, the Santa Fe Trail became a bustling trade route. Traffic increased during the Mexican-American War (1846–1848), when the trail became an important supply route. After the American victory, the Southwest became U.S. territory. Army forts along the trail ensured a steady demand for military supplies, and business continued to boom. The arrival of the transcontinental railroad in Santa Fe in 1880 proved to be the beginning of large-scale settlement of the Southwest. Trains replaced the Santa Fe Trail, as people and goods began to travel by rail.

Reading Time _____

Recalling Facts

1. In 1822 most of the Southwest was part of
   - ❏ a. Spain.
   - ❏ b. Mexico.
   - ❏ c. the United States.

2. William Becknell's second trade journey differed from his first in that on the second journey he
   - ❏ a. used pack horses rather than wagons.
   - ❏ b. made a profit in Santa Fe.
   - ❏ c. crossed the desert rather than the mountains.

3. On his second journey, Becknell found a water supply in
   - ❏ a. the Cimarron River.
   - ❏ b. the Colorado River.
   - ❏ c. the Arkansas River.

4. What made trade possible between Mexico and the United States was
   - ❏ a. Mexico's independence from Spain.
   - ❏ b. the Mexican-American War.
   - ❏ c. Becknell's discovery of a shorter route to Santa Fe.

5. On his second trip, Becknell's wagons were hauled by
   - ❏ a. mules.
   - ❏ b. horses.
   - ❏ c. oxen.

Understanding Ideas

6. Which of the following statements is a correct inference?
   - ❏ a. Traders waited until the Santa Fe Trail was established before traveling to the Southwest.
   - ❏ b. The Mexican-American War hurt trade in the Southwest.
   - ❏ c. People tend to travel to places where they can make money.

7. The most likely reason that the people of Santa Fe were willing to pay high prices for goods was that
   - ❏ a. they were wealthy.
   - ❏ b. goods were not available there.
   - ❏ c. they could resell them elsewhere at even higher prices.

8. The fact that most of the Santa Fe Trail traffic was on the desert route suggests that
   - ❏ a. saving time was worth risking a lack of water.
   - ❏ b. the desert was inhabited by people who welcomed travelers.
   - ❏ c. later travelers followed Native American trails.

9. The main factor that led to the establishment of the Santa Fe Trail was
   - ❏ a. the opening of the Mexican market to trade.
   - ❏ b. the need for supplies during the Mexican-American War.
   - ❏ c. the discovery of a water supply in the desert.

10. Becknell was called the Father of the Santa Fe Trail because he
   - ❏ a. almost died on his journey.
   - ❏ b. established the trail as a trade route.
   - ❏ c. discovered the trail.

17 B   Tejanos

Like all Southwestern states, Texas culture has a distinctly Mexican flavor. Despite their cultural influence, Tejanos, as Texans of Mexican descent are known, have suffered discrimination at the hands of the state's Anglo, or non-Hispanic, residents.

This was not always the case. While Texas was part of Mexico, Tejanos were independent ranchers. However, as Texas increased its ties with the United States—becoming a state in 1845—large numbers of settlers of European descent traveled there. Tejanos became a minority in their own state. They were pushed to the outskirts of financial and cultural life, and many had their lands unfairly seized. Since the 1800s, many Tejanos have occupied the lower rungs of the economic ladder. They have worked in hard jobs in farming, construction, ranching, and the service industry. Many have endured segregation and have been denied voting rights.

But Tejanos have retained their culture, much of which grew out of their ranching past. Their artisans make fine saddles, saddle blankets, and spurs. Their *conjunto* music, with its accordions and polka-like rhythms, is popular. Ceramics, woven goods, quilts, and yard altars are familiar Tejano folk arts. Perhaps the best known of their folk art objects are the lightweight, brightly adorned hollow sculptures called *piñatas*. At parties blindfolded children try to break open a *piñata* with a stick to reach the candy inside.

1. **Recognizing Words in Context**

   Find the word *discrimination* in the passage. One definition below is closest to the meaning of that word. One definition has the opposite or nearly the opposite meaning. The remaining definition has a completely different meaning. Label the definitions C for *closest*, O for *opposite or nearly opposite*, and D for *different*.

   _____ a. fairness

   _____ b. industry

   _____ c. bias

2. **Distinguishing Fact from Opinion**

   Two of the statements below present *facts*, which can be proved. The other statement is an *opinion*, which expresses someone's thoughts or beliefs. Label the statements F for *fact* and O for *opinion*.

   _____ a. Tejano *conjunto* music is similar to polka music.

   _____ b. Anglos who seized Tejano land should have gone to prison.

   _____ c. Tejano culture has been influential in Texas.

3. Keeping Events in Order

Number the statements below 1, 2, and 3 to show the order in which the events took place.

_____ a. Texas was part of Mexico.

_____ b. Tejano land was seized.

_____ c. Texas became part of the United States.

4. Making Correct Inferences

Two of the statements below are correct *inferences,* or reasonable guesses. They are based on information in the passage. The other statement is an incorrect, or faulty, inference. Label the statements C for *correct* inference and F for *faulty* inference.

_____ a. Tejano culture developed after settlement of people of European descent began in Texas.

_____ b. Arts and crafts are important in Tejano culture.

_____ c. Tejanos suffered increased discrimination when they became a minority.

5. Understanding Main Ideas

One of the statements below expresses the main idea of the passage. One statement is too general, or too broad. The other explains only part of the passage; it is too narrow. Label the statements M for *main idea,* B for *too broad,* and N for *too narrow.*

_____ a. Tejanos have made important cultural contributions in Texas despite being denied opportunities.

_____ b. Saddle making is a Tejano folk art that grew out of the ranching tradition.

_____ c. Texans of Mexican descent are known as Tejanos.

Correct Answers, Part A _____

Correct Answers, Part B _____

Total Correct Answers _____

Let the Play Begin!

Legend has it that the performing arts began when a Greek singer named Thespis invented tragedy. In 534 B.C., Thespis was performing a hymn to the god Dionysius. Such hymns, called dithyrambs, were usually sung by a lead singer and a chorus. Thespis added a speaking actor. Performances at the annual Dionysian festival soon included plays with three actors as well as the standard hymns. By 449 B.C., the Greeks were giving prizes to the best actor and the best playwright at the festival. A modern word for actor—*thespian*—recognizes the debt today's drama owes to Thespis.

Performing in a Greek play required stamina. Because each play had only three actors, performers had to play several roles. Chorus members both sang and danced. Being in the chorus for the many performances given at a festival was said to be as demanding as competing in the Olympic Games.

The Theater of Dionysius in Athens could hold 20,000 people. Even those in the front rows were quite a distance from the actors. Performers used grand gestures and wore masks so that they could be seen by everyone in their huge audience. Tragic actors wore dignified robes and masks that allowed clear speech. Comic actors wore short costumes that let them move freely and masks designed to make them look ugly or silly. Sometimes the chorus was costumed to look like animals. Although most actors no longer wear masks, dramas are still classified as tragedies or comedies, and special-effects makeup is still popular. Another tradition that survives from ancient Athens is political satire. Actors sometimes wore masks that made them look like well-known public figures. One was worn by the playwright Aristophanes. Aristophanes had a feud with the dictator Cleon and he wrote several plays attacking Cleon. Supposedly, the actors were all too afraid of Cleon to appear in Aristophanes' play *The Knights,* so the playwright played the role of the ruler himself.

Another legacy of the ancient Greeks is the deus ex machina, or "god of the machine." If a playwright was having trouble with the plot, he might have a god appear through a trap door. The god would rescue the main character and resolve any tricky plot situations. Modern writers might not call on divinities, but they do sometimes use unlikely ways to end a story. A character or an event that brings a complicated plot to an improbable conclusion is still called a deus ex machina.

Reading Time _____

Recalling Facts

1. Thespis is credited with having invented
   - ❏ a. singing.
   - ❏ b. dancing.
   - ❏ c. drama.

2. The most ancient of Greek plays had only _____ actors and a chorus.
   - ❏ a. two
   - ❏ b. one
   - ❏ c. four

3. In ancient Athens, plays were performed.
   - ❏ a. at the Olympic Games.
   - ❏ b. to honor the god Dionysius.
   - ❏ c. to celebrate a victory in battle.

4. Playwrights in ancient Athens wrote tragedies, comedies, and
   - ❏ a. satires.
   - ❏ b. musicals.
   - ❏ c. monologues.

5. A deus ex machina is
   - ❏ a. a kind of comic play involving ancient machines.
   - ❏ b. a disguise worn by an actor.
   - ❏ c. an unlikely character or event that untangles a plot.

Understanding Ideas

6. Early Greek actors wore masks to
   - ❏ a. glorify Dionysius instead of themselves.
   - ❏ b. make facial features of the characters visible in the huge theater.
   - ❏ c. keep their identities secret.

7. One difference between early Greek comedy and tragedy is that
   - ❏ a. visual symbols represented different moods.
   - ❏ b. tragic actors were more revered than comic actors.
   - ❏ c. comic plays drew larger audiences than tragedies.

8. One can infer from the passage that
   - ❏ a. Aristophanes and Cleon were friends who had differences of opinion.
   - ❏ b. Aristophanes' popularity may have protected him from Cleon's revenge.
   - ❏ c. most people respected their rulers too much to criticize them.

9. What is the best evidence that the Greeks enjoyed drama?
   - ❏ a. Plays required many performers.
   - ❏ b. Performances at the annual Dionysian festival included plays.
   - ❏ c. Prizes were awarded to the best actor and playwright.

10. Which statement best summarizes the passage?
    - ❏ a. Thespis was a singer in ancient Athens.
    - ❏ b. Early Greek drama influenced today's theater.
    - ❏ c. Political satire began in Greece.

The Fearless Comedy of Aristophanes

Everything known today about the early Greek comedies comes from the plays of one man, Aristophanes. The works of other comic writers from the fifth century B.C. have been lost, but 11 of Aristophanes' plays survive. His comedies often won first prize at the Dionysian festival, and they are still performed today.

The Acharnians is the earliest of his surviving comedies. Written during one of the many wars between Sparta and Athens, it has a main character who decides to make peace with the enemy. This play is considered the first antiwar comedy.

In *The Clouds,* the playwright takes on the famous philosopher Socrates. An old man enrolls in "Socrates' Thinking Shop" to learn to argue. He decides that his son would get more out of the lessons. The son then beats his father and uses Socratic arguments to justify his disrespect.

In *The Wasps,* Aristophanes attacks a favorite target—the legal system. An old man spends so much time watching trials that his son finally forces him to stay home. The old man is desperate to escape until his fellow jurors appear as a swarm of wasps to rescue him.

Aristophanes also invented satire. *The Knights* portrays the ruler of Athens, Cleon, as a dishonest dictator. Cleon took the playwright to court, but Aristophanes continued to satirize him in other plays.

1. **Recognizing Words in Context**

   Find the word *satirized* in the passage. One definition below is closest to the meaning of that word. One definition has the opposite or nearly the opposite meaning. The remaining definition has a completely different meaning. Label the definitions C for *closest,* O for *opposite or nearly opposite,* and D for *different.*

   _____ a. ridiculed

   _____ b. praised

   _____ c. excused

2. **Distinguishing Fact from Opinion**

   Two of the statements below present *facts,* which can be proved. The other statement is an *opinion,* which expresses someone's thoughts or beliefs. Label the statements F for *fact* and O for *opinion.*

   _____ a. Aristophanes lived in ancient Greece.

   _____ b. Aristophanes won many prizes for his comedies.

   _____ c. Aristophanes is the world's best writer of comedies.

3. Keeping Events in Order

Number the statements below 1, 2, and 3 to show the order in which the events took place.

_____ a. Cleon takes Aristophanes to court.

_____ b. Aristophanes writes *The Knights*.

_____ c. Aristophanes writes *The Acharnians*.

4. Making Correct Inferences

Two of the statements below are correct *inferences,* or reasonable guesses. They are based on information in the passage. The other statement is an incorrect, or faulty, inference. Label the statements C for *correct* inference and F for *faulty* inference.

_____ a. Aristophanes opposed the repeated wars between Athens and Sparta.

_____ b. Today's audiences do not find humor in the plays of Aristophanes.

_____ c. Aristophanes was an innovative playwright.

5. Understanding Main Ideas

One of the statements below expresses the main idea of the passage. One statement is too general, or too broad. The other explains only part of the passage; it is too narrow. Label the statements M for *main idea,* B for *too broad,* and N for *too narrow.*

_____ a. Aristophanes satirized Cleon, the ruler of Athens.

_____ b. Theater was an important art form in early Greece.

_____ c. The comic playwright Aristophanes fearlessly criticized Greek society and its leaders.

Correct Answers, Part A _____

Correct Answers, Part B _____

Total Correct Answers _____

Bicycle Use Around the World

In countries around the world, people ride bicycles. For some people, bicycles are recreational, but others use them as transportation. Bicycles are one of the most energy-efficient and cost-effective means of transportation. They need no fuel, are much less expensive than cars, and are easy to maneuver through crowded places.

More than 2,000 police departments in the United States have bicycle patrols, as do police departments in many other countries. One fully equipped police bike costs about $1,200. Compare that price to about $25,000 for a patrol car. Bicycle patrols are useful for policing areas such as parks and for zipping through crowded city streets.

Although only a small percentage of Americans use bicycles for transportation, bicycles are a major mode of transportation for people in other parts of the world, such as Asia. In many Asian cities, people use bicycles and foot-operated vehicles such as rickshaws and cyclos to transport paying customers or hundreds of pounds of freight. In some Chinese cities, bicycle trips account for more than half of all trips. Local governments in Japan built millions of bicycle parking spaces at train stations to encourage people to use bicycles instead of cars to reach the train station.

The bicycle is also widely used in Europe. The Netherlands is probably the country in which the bike is most widely used. There are many reasons for this. First, in the Netherlands, as in the rest of Europe, gasoline is very expensive. Second, most of the land is flat, which makes riding a bike there much easier than in countries with mountains and hills. Third, houses are often very close to businesses. This makes it easier for people to use bicycles to get to and from work. Perhaps most important, the Dutch government has built thousands of miles of bicycle paths and bike lanes. As a result, factory workers, farmers, shop owners, accountants, lawyers, and teachers ride bicycles to work.

In Africa people also often use bicycles. In some parts of Africa, programs have encouraged the use of bicycles as taxis to transport shoppers to markets, children to school, and sick people to medical facilities. A driver can transform a bicycle taxi into an ambulance by attaching a trailer to it.

Other means of transportation may come and go, but the bicycle, invented in the early nineteenth century, has clearly stood the test of time.

Reading Time _____

Recalling Facts

1. Bicycles are one of the
   - ❏ a. most cost-effective means of transportation.
   - ❏ b. most comfortable modes of transportation.
   - ❏ c. quickest ways to travel.

2. In many Asian cities, people use rickshaws and cyclos
   - ❏ a. primarily for recreation.
   - ❏ b. to transport people and freight.
   - ❏ c. mostly for national racing competitions.

3. In Japan, bicycle parking stations were built at train stations to encourage people to
   - ❏ a. use bicycles instead of trains.
   - ❏ b. use bicycles instead of cars to reach the train station.
   - ❏ c. get off their bicycles before entering crowded streets.

4. The Dutch government built thousands of
   - ❏ a. bicycle paths and bike lanes.
   - ❏ b. bicycles for mail carriers.
   - ❏ c. inexpensive bicycles.

5. A driver can transform a bicycle into an ambulance by
   - ❏ a. taking a sick person to a hospital.
   - ❏ b. paying a fee to the government.
   - ❏ c. attaching a trailer to it.

Understanding Ideas

6. One can infer from the passage that
   - ❏ a. bicycles are really best used by children.
   - ❏ b. the bicycle was an important invention.
   - ❏ c. bicycle use will soon diminish in popularity.

7. It is probable that American police departments
   - ❏ a. have abandoned the use of bicycle patrols.
   - ❏ b. consider bicycle patrols an unnecessary expense.
   - ❏ c. have found bicycle patrols useful.

8. Compared with Americans, the Dutch probably ride
   - ❏ a. their bicycles less.
   - ❏ b. ride their bicycles as much.
   - ❏ c. ride their bicycles more.

9. More Americans might ride bikes to work and school if
   - ❏ a. there were more bicycle paths.
   - ❏ b. gas were less expensive.
   - ❏ c. bicycles were less expensive.

10. One can conclude from the passage that using bicycles
    - ❏ a. costs less and pollutes less than using cars.
    - ❏ b. is less efficient than driving a car.
    - ❏ c. costs more but pollutes less than taking a train.

Military Uses of the Bicycle in World War II

World War II required massive movements of armies and supplies. Stealth was essential sometimes so that the enemy would not hear approaching troops, and sometimes moves were into places that were inaccessible by trucks and tanks. Cars, trucks, and tanks run on fuel, but often there was none. The bicycle solved these and other problems. It required no fuel, and it was quiet and easy to maneuver. Cyclists did not need regular roads, and they could go many places where trucks and tanks could not. Perhaps most important, a soldier could easily carry a lightweight bicycle.

Armies often used bicycles as transportation. For example, the Japanese successfully used whole troops of bicyclists in the Malay Peninsula and Singapore, among other places in Asia. Thousands of Japanese soldiers bicycled along roads, down narrow paths, and along jungle trails to surround and defeat the British.

In Europe the German army sent bicycle troops ahead of their tanks to battle the Norwegian army. They knew that bikes could cross the steep Norway landscape more easily than tanks could. One night British soldiers parachuted into German-occupied France, quickly assembled bikes they had brought, and then sped silently away to destroy a radar station. Thus, this simple machine, the bicycle, was an important tool during World War II.

1. **Recognizing Words in Context**

   Find the word *stealth* in the passage. One definition below is closest to the meaning of that word. One definition has the opposite or nearly the opposite meaning. The remaining definition has a completely different meaning. Label the definitions C for *closest,* O for *opposite or nearly opposite,* and D for *different.*

   _____ a. openness

   _____ b. pride

   _____ c. secrecy

2. **Distinguishing Fact from Opinion**

   Two of the statements below present *facts,* which can be proved. The other statement is an *opinion,* which expresses someone's thoughts or beliefs. Label the statements F for *fact* and O for *opinion.*

   _____ a. Armies used bicycles as transportation.

   _____ b. Bicycles were the best kind of transportation for armies.

   _____ c. German bicycle troops could cross Norwegian slopes more easily than tanks could.

3. Keeping Events in Order

Number the statements below 1, 2, and 3 to show the order in which the events took place.

_____ a. British soldiers assembled bikes.

_____ b. British soldiers destroyed a radar station.

_____ c. British soldiers parachuted into enemy territory.

4. Making Correct Inferences

Two of the statements below are correct *inferences,* or reasonable guesses. They are based on information in the passage. The other statement is an incorrect, or faulty, inference. Label the statements C for *correct* inference and F for *faulty* inference.

_____ a. Without bikes, the British could not have destroyed a radar station.

_____ b. Having bicycles made it easier for the Germans to invade Norway.

_____ c. When fuel was unavailable, soldiers probably used bikes if they had them.

5. Understanding Main Ideas

One of the statements below expresses the main idea of the passage. One statement is too general, or too broad. The other explains only part of the passage; it is too narrow. Label the statements M for *main idea,* B for *too broad,* and N for *too narrow.*

_____ a. Bicycles were useful in certain military situations during World War II.

_____ b. Transporting troops by bicycle was part of the Japanese military strategy in the Malay Peninsula.

_____ c. Armies have frequently used bicycles instead of other vehicles in wartime.

Correct Answers, Part A _____

Correct Answers, Part B _____

Total Correct Answers _____

The Conquests of Hernando Cortés

In 1519 Spanish explorer Hernando Cortés led an expedition to Mexico to gain land and gold for the Spanish Empire. Taking the route of an earlier explorer, Cortés sailed to the Yucatán. There he conquered the people of Tabasco. From them he learned about the wealthy Aztec Empire ruled by Montezuma. One of his captives, Malinche, knew both the Mayan and Aztec languages. Malinche became Cortés's interpreter and guide.

After sailing farther up the coast, Cortés landed and founded the first Spanish settlement in Mexico, today called Veracruz. There he met messengers from Montezuma, who brought Cortés gold and gifts. They also suggested that Cortés leave Mexico immediately. Cortés, however, was eager to capture the city from which such valuable gifts came, so he began his march inland to the Aztec capital, Tenochtitlán. Malinche had told Cortés about the many Native American peoples who disliked the Aztecs. Thus, along the way, Cortés formed an alliance with the Tlaxcalans, whom Montezuma had tried to conquer for many years.

Montezuma, meanwhile, listened to his messengers describe the appearance of the Spaniards and the odd weapon Cortés had fired. The Aztecs had never seen a gun, nor had they seen people on horseback. Montezuma thought that Cortés might be the god Quetzalcoatl, who had left earth long ago but was expected to return to claim his kingdom in 1519.

Although at first hesitant, Montezuma invited Cortés into the capital. There Cortés saw vast amounts of gold and other treasures. Afraid that the Aztecs would kill him and his forces, Cortés took Montezuma hostage. While Cortés ruled the Aztecs through Montezuma, his forces melted gold to prepare it for shipment to Spain.

After a brief absence in the spring of 1520, Cortés returned to Tenochtitlán, where he found that the man he had left in charge had killed many Aztecs. The Aztecs attacked Cortés and his followers. Montezuma was killed during the battle, and most of Cortés's forces were killed as they tried to escape. Cortés and his remaining forces fled to Tlaxcala.

The next year, after gathering together many Native American allies, Cortés attacked Tenochtitlán. After several months, the last Aztec ruler surrendered. Cortés, continuing his conquests, explored parts of Central America and sent expeditions to conquer the rest of the Aztec Empire. Before long Cortés the conqueror had destroyed the Aztec Empire and claimed its lands for Spain.

Reading Time _____

Recalling Facts

1. Hernando Cortés first conquered the people of
   - ❑ a. Tlaxcala.
   - ❑ b. Veracruz.
   - ❑ c. Tabasco.

2. Cortés went to Mexico in
   - ❑ a. 1519.
   - ❑ b. 1520.
   - ❑ c. 1521.

3. According to one story, Montezuma thought that Cortés might be
   - ❑ a. Malintzin.
   - ❑ b. Tlaxcala.
   - ❑ c. Quetzalcoatl.

4. In 1521 Cortés attacked
   - ❑ a. Montezuma.
   - ❑ b. the people of Tabasco.
   - ❑ c. Tenochtitlán.

5. Cortés claimed the lands of the Aztec Empire for
   - ❑ a. himself.
   - ❑ b. Spain.
   - ❑ c. Malinche.

Understanding Ideas

6. According to the information in the passage, it is likely that the Yucatán is in
   - ❑ a. Spain.
   - ❑ b. Mexico.
   - ❑ c. Veracruz.

7. Montezuma's religious beliefs made him
   - ❑ a. think he was invincible.
   - ❑ b. a peaceful and loving leader.
   - ❑ c. afraid to fight Cortez.

8. At first the Aztecs refrained from attacking Cortés and his followers, probably because they
   - ❑ a. feared that Cortés would kill Montezuma.
   - ❑ b. were a peace-loving people.
   - ❑ c. were not powerful enough to win.

9. Without Malinche it is possible that Cortés
   - ❑ a. might not have defeated the Aztecs.
   - ❑ b. would not have sailed to the Yucatán.
   - ❑ c. might not have received gifts from Montezuma.

10. One can conclude from the passage that the Tlaxcalans
    - ❑ a. were related to Malinche.
    - ❑ b. were necessary to Cortés's conquering the Aztecs.
    - ❑ c. tried to convince Cortés to leave Mexico.

The current national flag of Mexico is similar to the one that was adopted in 1821 after Mexico won freedom from Spain. Both flags are tricolor with vertical stripes of green, white, and red. The three stripes are symbolic, representing the "three guarantees," or three promises, that Mexican leaders made to unite the people in their struggle for freedom from Spain. The green stripe stands for independence, the white stripe for religion, and the red stripe for union.

The Mexican coat of arms appears on the white stripe. At times officials have altered the appearance of the coat of arms. It symbolizes the Aztec origins of Mexico City. According to legend, the Aztec god Huitzilopochtli directed the Aztecs to settle where they saw an eagle perched on a cactus, eating a snake. In about 1325, the Aztecs found the place that Huitzilopochtli had described and began to build their capital city, Tenochtitlán.

On the earlier flag, a crowned eagle is standing on a cactus. On today's flag, an uncrowned eagle holding a snake is standing on a cactus. The cactus is growing from a rock surrounded by water, and a half circle of oak and laurel branches surrounds the bottom of the emblem.

Thus, old or new, the national flags of Mexico represent similar historic events.

1. **Recognizing Words in Context**

Find the word *altered* in the passage. One definition below is closest to the meaning of that word. One definition has the opposite or nearly the opposite meaning. The remaining definition has a completely different meaning. Label the definitions C for *closest*, O for *opposite or nearly opposite*, and D for *different*.

_____ a. changed

_____ b. alerted

_____ c. retained

2. **Distinguishing Fact from Opinion**

Two of the statements below present *facts*, which can be proved. The other statement is an *opinion*, which expresses someone's thoughts or beliefs. Label the statements F for *fact* and O for *opinion*.

_____ a. The story of the Mexican flag is a fascinating legend.

_____ b. The green band on the Mexican flag represents independence.

_____ c. Mexico's current national flag is similar to one adopted in 1821.

3. Keeping Events in Order

Number the statements below 1, 2, and 3 to show the order in which the events took place.

_____ a. The Mexican flag was designed and adopted.

_____ b. Huitzilopochtli directed the Aztecs to settle where they saw an eagle on a cactus, eating a snake.

_____ c. The Aztecs started building Tenochtitlán.

4. Making Correct Inferences

Two of the statements below are correct *inferences,* or reasonable guesses. They are based on information in the passage. The other statement is an incorrect, or faulty, inference. Label the statements C for *correct* inference and F for *faulty* inference.

_____ a. The legend of the founding of Tenochtitlán has been known in Mexico for hundreds of years.

_____ b. Tenochtitlán eventually became Mexico City.

_____ c. The changes made to the Mexican coat of arms probably have no meaning.

5. Understanding Main Ideas

One of the statements below expresses the main idea of the passage. One statement is too general, or too broad. The other explains only part of the passage; it is too narrow. Label the statements M for *main idea,* B for *too broad,* and N for *too narrow.*

_____ a. Flags are symbolic.

_____ b. The Mexican flag has three stripes: one green, one white, and one red.

_____ c. Both national flags of Mexico contain elements that represent similar historic events.

Correct Answers, Part A _____

Correct Answers, Part B _____

Total Correct Answers _____

Cultures have long known that human life tends to progress in stages—birth, childhood, adulthood, marriage, parenthood, and death. To mark the passage between these stages, people often conduct rituals called "rites of passage." One such rite is for coming of age. This is the point at which childhood is thought to end and adulthood to begin. It has often been celebrated with complex community-wide rituals.

In today's Western world, modern customs have largely replaced such rituals. Getting a driver's license, attending a senior prom, and graduating from high school are among the few coming-of-age ceremonies that many U.S. teenagers experience. However, some religions still provide young members with the option of taking part in a formal coming-of-age rite of passage.

A rite of passage has three main phases: separation, liminality, and incorporation. The three phases are marked by symbolic activities. In Roman Catholic Latin American cultures, many girls go through a ceremony called *quinceañera* on their fifteenth birthday. A special Mass identifies the girl as an adult member of the church. During the reception that follows, the girl's father enacts his daughter's symbolic separation from childhood. He removes her flat shoes and places high-heeled shoes on her feet to symbolize her adulthood and readiness for courtship.

The Amish have a unique way of acting out liminality in a coming-of-age ritual. Liminality is an in-between state in which people are not bound by the usual rules of their society. Among the Amish, baptism is celebrated in the late teen years. It represents a person's free choice to join the church as an adult. To prepare teenagers for this event, the Amish have a tradition called *rumspringa,* or "running around." During *rumspringa,* 16-year-olds are allowed to behave in ways that are normally forbidden by the Amish religion, such as attending parties, riding around in cars, and staying out late. The Amish believe that only after experiencing such activities can young people choose to give them up.

The bar mitzvah is another rite marking the beginning of religious adulthood. In a bar mitzvah rite, a 13-year-old Jewish boy signals his adulthood by leading his congregation in parts of the Sabbath service. The bar mitzvah is the public acknowledgment of a young man's new role in the Jewish faith. It helps to prepare him for the activities, rights, and duties that this role will entail.

Reading Time _____

Recalling Facts

1. A ceremony or ritual marking the transition from one stage of life to the next is called
   - ❏ a. liminality.
   - ❏ b. a rite of passage.
   - ❏ c. rumspringa.

2. The bar mitzvah is a coming-of-age rite in the
   - ❏ a. Latin American community.
   - ❏ b. Jewish faith.
   - ❏ c. Amish faith.

3. Which rite of passage is characterized by rule breaking?
   - ❏ a. *quinceañera*
   - ❏ b. bar mitzvah
   - ❏ c. *rumspringa*

4. The three main phases of a rite of passage are
   - ❏ a. separation, liminality, and incorporation.
   - ❏ b. acknowledgment, rule breaking, and coming of age.
   - ❏ c. preparation, ceremony, and baptism.

5. Typical life stages for people in all cultures include
   - ❏ a. birth, career, and death.
   - ❏ b. adolescence, parenthood, and retirement.
   - ❏ c. adulthood, parenthood, and death.

Understanding Ideas

6. Coming of age in Amish tradition is distinguished by its
   - ❏ a. emphasis on free choice.
   - ❏ b. tradition of incorporation.
   - ❏ c. acceptance of parties.

7. Which of the following is an illustration of the public function of a rite of passage?
   - ❏ a. Amish young people choose to accept baptism.
   - ❏ b. A Jewish boy feels a new sense of kinship with other Jews after his bar mitzvah.
   - ❏ c. After a girl's *quinceañera,* boys know that they may ask her for a date.

8. One can conclude that
   - ❏ a. rites of passage are not so important today.
   - ❏ b. life stages are different today.
   - ❏ c. coming of age is significant to the individual and the community.

9. For the Amish, rule breaking serves what purpose?
   - ❏ a. It allows young people to delay adulthood.
   - ❏ b. It prepares young people to reject such behavior.
   - ❏ c. It teaches young people humility.

10. Coming-of-age rites of passage are important because
    - ❏ a. young people receive presents.
    - ❏ b. they help young people to understand and acknowledge their new roles as adults.
    - ❏ c. they give young people the right to take part in adult activities.

The *quinceañera,* fifteenth-birthday celebration, is a special event in the lives of many girls of Latin American descent. A *quinceañera* can often be as elaborate as a wedding. The parents, with the help of sponsors, buy the honoree's white or pastel dress. They order a cake and flowers, hire caterers, buy gifts and party favors, and plan decorations. They also reserve the reception hall and arrange for music. The girl selects a theme and chooses her escort and court of honor, which may include up to 14 couples.

The *quinceañera* generally begins with the *misa de acción de gracias,* or thanksgiving Mass, which marks the girl's commitment to Christian ideals. Afterward, the guests gather for a reception. A typical reception begins with the introduction of the honoree and the guests of honor. The girl's father or a male guardian then changes her shoes from flats to high heels. An honored female friend or relative places a tiara on her head. The girl may then give or receive a doll, symbolizing the last doll of her childhood. She and her father or guardian dance a waltz, which is followed by a rehearsed and choreographed dance performance by the entire court of honor. The parents or godparents offer a toast, the guests enjoy a traditional meal, and dancing and merrymaking continue until late.

1. **Recognizing Words in Context**

   Find the word *choreographed* in the passage. One definition below is closest to the meaning of that word. One definition has the opposite or nearly the opposite meaning. The remaining definition has a completely different meaning. Label the definitions C for *closest,* O for *opposite or nearly opposite,* and D for *different.*

   _____ a. computerized

   _____ b. unplanned

   _____ c. arranged

2. **Distinguishing Fact from Opinion**

   Two of the statements below present *facts,* which can be proved. The other statement is an *opinion,* which expresses someone's thoughts or beliefs. Label the statements F for *fact* and O for *opinion.*

   _____ a. At her *quinceañera,* a girl may give or receive a doll.

   _____ b. Although planning a *quinceañera* is hard work, the memories it provides are always worthwhile.

   _____ c. The court of honor at a *quinceañera* may include as many as 14 couples.

3. Keeping Events in Order

Number the statements below 1, 2, and 3 to show the order in which the events took place.

_____ a. A thanksgiving Mass is celebrated.

_____ b. The honoree chooses her court of honor.

_____ c. The young woman dances a waltz with her father or guardian.

4. Making Correct Inferences

Two of the statements below are correct *inferences,* or reasonable guesses. They are based on information in the passage. The other statement is an incorrect, or faulty, inference. Label the statements C for *correct* inference and F for *faulty* inference.

_____ a. A *quinceañera* may be an expensive event.

_____ b. A girl who has had a *quinceañera* begins to act maturely after the celebration.

_____ c. Sponsors play an important role in planning and hosting a *quinceañera.*

5. Understanding Main Ideas

One of the statements below expresses the main idea of the passage. One statement is too general, or too broad. The other explains only part of the passage; it is too narrow. Label the statements M for *main idea,* B for *too broad,* and N for *too narrow.*

_____ a. A *quinceañera* is a rite-of-passage celebration for Latin American girls that includes a thanksgiving Mass and an elaborate reception.

_____ b. A rite of passage, such as a *quinceañera,* marks a significant transition in a girl's life.

_____ c. Changing shoes symbolizes the passage into adulthood in a *quinceañera.*

Correct Answers, Part A _____

Correct Answers, Part B _____

Total Correct Answers _____

Hong Kong: The World's Freest Economy

Since 1996 economists working with the Fraser Institute of Canada have published an economic-freedom index. Each year they rate the financial systems of up to 125 countries and regions. The index gives high scores to countries with nonfluctuating money values, respect for property rights, and few barriers to global trade. The United States generally ranks among the highest-scoring nations, but the top score—and the title of the "world's freest economy"—consistently goes to Hong Kong.

The region's openness to trade began when the British took control in the 1840s. Previously the Chinese had tried to limit trade with the West. Foreigners were allowed to do business only in the city of Canton, and goods imported from the West were heavily taxed. British companies bought large amounts of tea from China, but China purchased little from the British. The resulting trade imbalance hurt the British economy. Britain's trying to force China to remove its barriers to trade led to the Opium Wars. In 1842 Britain gained control of the island of Hong Kong after winning the first war. In 1898 China leased the nearby New Territories to Britain for 99 years.

Under British rule, Hong Kong grew from a barren island into the business center of Asia. After Hong Kong became a free-trade zone, the region began to develop its geographic advantages. Removing barriers to trade made Hong Kong one of the world's busiest ports. Hong Kong includes the New Territories in southern China, which produce 40 percent of China's exports. Its deep harbor can hold the world's largest ships.

The free-market policy established by the British continues today. Hong Kong's government imposes no quotas on the amount of goods brought into or shipped out of Hong Kong. Taxes are kept to a minimum. Residents may invest their money abroad without restriction, and foreign companies are encouraged to invest in Hong Kong. This free-market policy has made Hong Kong a center of finance as well as of trade.

When Britain's lease expired in 1997, many feared that China's Communist government would attempt to regulate Hong Kong's economy. However, as a Special Administrative Region (SAR) of the People's Republic of China, Hong Kong is governed under the "one nation—two systems" philosophy. On the mainland, the central government owns the most important resources and plans the economy, but Hong Kong's free-market system is to remain unchanged until 2047, 50 years after its return to China.

Reading Time _____

Recalling Facts

1. Hong Kong has been named the "world's freest economy" by the
   - ❑ a. United Nations.
   - ❑ b. Fraser Institute.
   - ❑ c. U.S. Department of Commerce.

2. For years economists have given Hong Kong high scores on the
   - ❑ a. economic-freedom index.
   - ❑ b. population-growth graph.
   - ❑ c. Human Development Index.

3. Hong Kong is a center of international trade and
   - ❑ a. mining.
   - ❑ b. oil refining.
   - ❑ c. finance.

4. Hong Kong was returned to the People's Republic of China after
   - ❑ a. Britain's lease expired in 1997.
   - ❑ b. its residents approved China's request to annex the region.
   - ❑ c. China promised to build a new international airport.

5. After its return to China, Hong Kong became
   - ❑ a. a province.
   - ❑ b. an independent country.
   - ❑ c. a special administrative region.

Understanding Ideas

6. With a free market-trade policy in Hong Kong,
   - ❑ a. the city's economy has flourished.
   - ❑ b. Britain's import and export trading became imbalanced, affecting its economy negatively.
   - ❑ c. there has been little change in its economy.

7. One geographic advantage that helped Hong Kong become an international trade center is its
   - ❑ a. abundant natural resources.
   - ❑ b. large airport.
   - ❑ c. deep harbor.

8. Hong Kong's free-market policy results in the government's
   - ❑ a. avoiding taxation of imports and exports.
   - ❑ b. restricting foreign investment.
   - ❑ c. limiting the amount of goods imported from abroad.

9. Although Hong Kong's government does not regulate the economy, it does maintain
   - ❑ a. steady emigration rates.
   - ❑ b. a stable financial and legal system.
   - ❑ c. strict wage controls.

10. One can conclude from the passage that the People's Republic of China
    - ❑ a. wants to change Hong Kong's economy to a communist system.
    - ❑ b. finds it advantageous to maintain Hong Kong's free-market economy.
    - ❑ c. intends for Hong Kong to become independent.

The Interest in Learning English in China

Since Hong Kong's return to China, interest in learning English has grown throughout the country. Industrious young Chinese want to learn how to use English in everyday situations so that they can get jobs with Western corporations that are investing in China.

Opportunities to learn English seem to be everywhere. Preschoolers in Beijing are learning words such as *apple* as they begin to walk. Students in Shanghai broadcast programs in English on their high schools' radio stations. Principals in Hong Kong are hiring native English speakers to teach in the region's school system. Beijing police are learning English to help them deal with the increasing number of foreign tourists. Throughout China, adults are investing more than $1 billion a year in classes, software programs, and tapes that teach English.

This interest in learning English marks a shift in the Chinese government's attitude about foreign trade. Before 1842 China tried to isolate itself from the West. European traders could conduct business only in the port of Canton. In 1842 the British won the Opium War and opened Hong Kong and other ports to trade. Now China is eager to attract foreign investment. In 2001 the country became a member of the World Trade Organization. Interest in English was also fueled by China's successful bid to host the 2008 Olympics.

1. **Recognizing Words in Context**

   Find the word *industrious* in the passage. One definition below is closest to the meaning of that word. One definition has the opposite or nearly the opposite meaning. The remaining definition has a completely different meaning. Label the definitions C for *closest*, O for *opposite or nearly opposite*, and D for *different*.

   _____ a. obvious

   _____ b. ambitious

   _____ c. sluggish

2. **Distinguishing Fact from Opinion**

   Two of the statements below present *facts*, which can be proved. The other statement is an *opinion*, which expresses someone's thoughts or beliefs. Label the statements F for *fact* and O for *opinion*.

   _____ a. Students should begin learning a foreign language in preschool.

   _____ b. Interest in learning English has created a huge market for instructional materials.

   _____ c. Hong Kong schools are hiring native English speakers.

3. Keeping Events in Order

Number the statements below 1, 2, and 3 to show the order in which the events took place.

_____ a. Hong Kong became a trading center.

_____ b. China joined the World Trade Organization.

_____ c. Britain and China fought the Opium War.

4. Making Correct Inferences

Two of the statements below are correct *inferences*, or reasonable guesses. They are based on information in the passage. The other statement is an incorrect, or faulty, inference. Label the statements C for *correct* inference and F for *faulty* inference.

_____ a. The interest in learning English in China marks a shift away from national pride.

_____ b. Relations between China and the West continue to change.

_____ c. Chinese students see learning English as a way to get ahead.

5. Understanding Main Ideas

One of the statements below expresses the main idea of the passage. One statement is too general, or too broad. The other explains only part of the passage; it is too narrow. Label the statements M for *main idea*, B for *too broad*, and N for *too narrow*.

_____ a. The English language is spoken by many nonnative speakers.

_____ b. Preschoolers in Beijing are learning to speak English.

_____ c. Growing foreign-trade opportunities have sparked interest throughout China in learning English.

Correct Answers, Part A _____

Correct Answers, Part B _____

Total Correct Answers _____

The Gullah are American descendents of enslaved Africans, most of whom came from rice-growing areas in West Africa. Many historians think that *Gullah* is derived from "Angola," an African country from which many enslaved people were shipped. Most Gullah live in the southeastern United States on the Sea Islands or along the coast of South Carolina and Georgia.

In the 1700s, after learning that a semitropical climate was ideal for growing rice, many white plantation owners in coastal South Carolina and Georgia became eager to cultivate this valuable cash crop. However, they did not know how to grow rice. Therefore, they made use of enslaved Africans who had the skills they lacked.

The enslaved Africans maintained many of their cultural traditions and handed them down to their children and grandchildren, just as many newcomers to the United States do today. They passed on recipes for rice dishes, made sweet-grass baskets, told folktales, and sang songs like those of their African ancestors. They placed plates and glasses on top of graves so that the dead would have vessels to eat and drink from in the hereafter.

Historians speculate that the Gullah were able to keep many of their traditions intact because of their isolation on the plantations. To avoid the heat and high level of disease on the plantations, landowners often lived elsewhere while their slaves worked the land. Freed during the Civil War, many Gullah remained on the Sea Islands and became landowners. Later generations of Gullah continued to farm the land.

Beginning in the mid-1900s, construction crews began to build roads to connect many of the Sea Islands to the mainland. Developers constructed luxury resorts and golf courses. Vacationers came to the islands to enjoy sandy beaches and ocean waves. Some Gullah sold their land to developers. Over time, property taxes increased, and soon the taxes were too high for many longtime Gullah residents to pay. Then they, too, sold their homes and land.

Although some extended families continue to live in homes that are clustered together—much as their African ancestors would have lived, albeit in modern houses—many people worry that the Gullah culture will vanish. Some Gullah feel that the best way to save their culture is to halt development. Others are educating government officials and even the United Nations about the Gullah traditions. They are determined to keep their centuries-old culture alive.

Reading Time _____

Recalling Facts

1. The Gullah culture developed
   - ❑ a. on the Sea Islands or along the coast of South Carolina and Georgia.
   - ❑ b. in various rice-growing countries.
   - ❑ c. among various West African tribes.

2. The Gullah are descended from enslaved people who came mostly from
   - ❑ a. Ethiopia.
   - ❑ b. West Africa.
   - ❑ c. South Africa.

3. The Gullah probably were able to maintain many traditions because
   - ❑ a. plantation owners liked the traditions.
   - ❑ b. they were fairly isolated on the rice plantations.
   - ❑ c. they were paid well by developers.

4. Many Gullah sold their homes and land when
   - ❑ a. vacationers came to the islands.
   - ❑ b. the Civil War ended.
   - ❑ c. taxes became too high for them to afford.

5. Some Gullah want to save their culture by
   - ❑ a. stopping development.
   - ❑ b. raising taxes.
   - ❑ c. relocating elsewhere.

Understanding Ideas

6. One can infer from the passage that uncontrolled development of the Sea Islands might
   - ❑ a. bring additional income to the Gullah.
   - ❑ b. be incompatible with the Gullah culture.
   - ❑ c. increase interest in the Gullah culture.

7. It is likely that the Gullah
   - ❑ a. feel a strong connection to their African heritage.
   - ❑ b. are comfortable with the changes taking place around them.
   - ❑ c. worry that development is occurring too slowly.

8. Compared with the Gullah of the 1700s, the Gullah today
   - ❑ a. are less isolated.
   - ❑ b. eat more rice.
   - ❑ c. own more land.

9. One can conclude from the passage that the Gullah
   - ❑ a. vacation at the island resorts.
   - ❑ b. are hesitant about talking to government officials.
   - ❑ c. are working to keep their culture from vanishing.

10. Had the plantation owners of coastal South Carolina and Georgia known how to grow rice, it is possible that
    - ❑ a. the Gullah culture would not have developed.
    - ❑ b. they would have grown other crops.
    - ❑ c. resorts would have been developed sooner.

23 B A Language Born of Need

The Gullah Creole language developed on rice plantations on the Sea Islands during the 1700s and 1800s. Plantation owners brought enslaved Africans to work on the farms. There the slaves learned that they lacked a common language. Needing to speak with one another and their English-speaking overseers, the slaves developed Gullah, a language they could all understand. Many of these enslaved Africans were from Sierra Leone. As a result, Gullah includes many words that come from languages spoken in that country. Gullah also includes influences from English and other West African languages.

Because Gullah came about from a need to understand spoken language, it is not surprising that Gullah developed as an oral language. Hence, there are no spelling rules for writing it. Instead, when people write Gullah, they use phonetic spellings, writing the sounds they hear to spell the words.

Some people have incorrectly identified Gullah as a dialect. Others mistakenly believe it to be African American slang or poorly spoken English. However, linguists confidently point out that Gullah has the three characteristics that make it a language: a grammatical structure, a sound pattern, and words. Speakers of Gullah also use idioms, forms that help make it a colorful language. Like all languages, Gullah will change as its speakers add new words and meanings to their language.

1. **Recognizing Words in Context**

   Find the word *grammatical* in the passage. One definition below is closest to the meaning of that word. One definition has the opposite or nearly the opposite meaning. The remaining definition has a completely different meaning. Label the definitions C for *closest,* O for *opposite or nearly opposite,* and D for *different.*

   _____ a. irregular

   _____ b. organized

   _____ c. strange

2. **Distinguishing Fact from Opinion**

   Two of the statements below present *facts,* which can be proved. The other statement is an *opinion,* which expresses someone's thoughts or beliefs. Label the statements F for *fact* and O for *opinion.*

   _____ a. Three characteristics make Gullah a language.

   _____ b. Gullah includes words from English and West African languages.

   _____ c. Gullah is beautiful when spoken.

3. Keeping Events in Order

Number the statements below 1, 2, and 3 to show the order in which the events took place.

_____ a. Enslaved Africans on the Sea Islands discovered that they lacked a common language.

_____ b. Enslaved Africans were brought to work on rice plantations on the Sea Islands.

_____ c. Enslaved Africans on the Sea Islands developed Gullah.

4. Making Correct Inferences

Two of the statements below are correct *inferences,* or reasonable guesses. They are based on information in the passage. The other statement is an incorrect, or faulty, inference. Label the statements C for *correct* inference and F for *faulty* inference.

_____ a. Enslaved Africans contributed words from their languages to develop Gullah.

_____ b. Two people might spell a Gullah word differently, but both will pronounce it the same way.

_____ c. It is easier to learn Gullah than to learn English.

5. Understanding Main Ideas

One of the statements below expresses the main idea of the passage. One statement is too general, or too broad. The other explains only part of the passage; it is too narrow. Label the statements M for *main idea,* B for *too broad,* and N for *too narrow.*

_____ a. There are many examples of languages that have developed orally.

_____ b. Gullah developed as a common language between West Africans and English speakers.

_____ c. Gullah is full of idioms.

Correct Answers, Part A _____

Correct Answers, Part B _____

Total Correct Answers _____

24 A   Competition for Water in the American West

The American West is a large region. It stretches from the middle of North Dakota to the middle of Texas at its eastern edge, and it is bounded to the west by the Pacific Ocean. In this area, water is a very precious resource. The West receives an average of only 20 inches of precipitation per year—not enough to support farms or large cities. Also, the precipitation is not spread evenly through the region. For example, coastal Oregon and Washington receive a lot of rain, but many parts of the Southwest and California are deserts. These normally dry areas may receive bursts of heavy rain but then go for months with little or no rain.

This all-or-nothing nature of precipitation, along with rapid regional growth, makes it difficult to meet competing demands for water. Urban areas need water for homes, offices, shopping centers, and recreational uses. Big businesses—whether agricultural, mining, or manufacturing—require large amounts of water.

In the past, huge storage dams served as reservoirs to capture as much precipitation as possible. In addition, water was pumped from ancient natural underground pools called *aquifers*. These earlier solutions caused new problems. Overuse caused many aquifers to run dry. Building so many dams—blocking rivers and streams that once flowed freely—also has had harmful effects on the environment. For example, the dams prevent salmon from swimming upstream to their spawning grounds.

Traditionally, there have been two conflicting systems of water rights. The doctrine of riparian rights states that water belongs to all who own land along a river or other water source. The doctrine of appropriated rights states that water belongs to those who have first used the water, no matter how far away the water is.

Native Americans are a special group in the struggle for water rights. Until the 1960s, their claims to water rights on their lands were largely ignored. Now the courts are recognizing many of those claims.

New solutions include the idea of creating a water market where farmers might sell water rights on their land for urban use. Farmers would receive more money for selling water than for growing crops. Because an acre of urban land requires less water than an acre of irrigated farmland, more water would be available for cities. Conservation is another important strategy receiving attention. Ideas range from homeowners' using low-flow toilets and showerheads to manufacturers' recycling wastewater.

Reading Time _____

Recalling Facts

1. The average annual precipitation in the West is
   - ❏ a. 30 inches.
   - ❏ b. 20 inches.
   - ❏ c. 10 inches.

2. Underground reservoirs of water are called
   - ❏ a. aquifers.
   - ❏ b. dams.
   - ❏ c. water rights.

3. Building dams creates
   - ❏ a. recycled water.
   - ❏ b. reservoirs.
   - ❏ c. a water market.

4. The doctrine that says water belongs to those who live near a river is the doctrine of
   - ❏ a. water market rights.
   - ❏ b. appropriated rights.
   - ❏ c. riparian rights.

5. The concept of a water market includes the idea of
   - ❏ a. businesses' recycling their wastewater for use by golf courses.
   - ❏ b. water's being used for cities rather than for farming.
   - ❏ c. the selling of water accumulated in reservoirs.

Understanding Ideas

6. From reading the passage, one can conclude that
   - ❏ a. Oregon has a dry climate.
   - ❏ b. Arizona has a dry climate.
   - ❏ c. the climate in all regions in the West is the same.

7. The water that is captured in reservoirs
   - ❏ a. is a good place for salmon to live.
   - ❏ b. increases the amount of water available to cities.
   - ❏ c. is not used for irrigation.

8. A city that draws its water supply from a river 200 miles away relies on
   - ❏ a. riparian rights.
   - ❏ b. Native American rights.
   - ❏ c. appropriated rights.

9. Creation of a water market would
   - ❏ a. have an impact on the farming economy.
   - ❏ b. benefit only farmers.
   - ❏ c. have no impact on cities.

10. From reading the passage, one can conclude that
    - ❏ a. the Western salmon population is declining.
    - ❏ b. Western salmon are reproducing in new areas.
    - ❏ c. salmon are the only species affected by dam construction.

24 B   The Designer of Los Angeles's Water Supply

Born in 1855, William Mulholland rose from humble beginnings to become head of the Los Angeles Water Department. He began his career there as a ditch digger on the Los Angeles River. After work Mulholland taught himself hydraulic engineering. Within eight years, he was a superintendent.

Knowing that the Los Angeles River would not be able to support the city's growing population, Mulholland looked to the larger Owens River, more than 200 miles away, as a source of water. He planned to build an aqueduct—a combination of canals, tunnels, and pipelines—to carry the water from high in the Sierra Nevada across the desert to the city located near sea level.

First, he needed to procure land and water rights from the farmers in the Owens River Valley. The farmers had been hoping for a large federal irrigation project for their land. However, Mulholland convinced the government to support his plan instead. Through a combination of hard work and some politics, Los Angeles soon owned the rights to most of the water in the valley.

The building of the aqueduct took more than five years. It was the largest American engineering project up to that time. Mulholland directed thousands of workers. In 1913 the people of Los Angeles received their first fresh water from the Owens River.

1. Recognizing Words in Context

Find the word *procure* in the passage. One definition below is closest to the meaning of that word. One definition has the opposite or nearly the opposite meaning. The remaining definition has a completely different meaning. Label the definitions C for *closest*, O for *opposite or nearly opposite*, and D for *different*.

_____ a. build

_____ b. acquire

_____ c. lose

2. Distinguishing Fact from Opinion

Two of the statements below present *facts*, which can be proved. The other statement is an *opinion*, which expresses someone's thoughts or beliefs. Label the statements F for *fact* and O for *opinion*.

_____ a. The Owens River aqueduct carried water more than 200 miles.

_____ b. The Owens River aqueduct was the best way for Los Angeles to get water.

_____ c. Los Angeles received water from the Owens River aqueduct in 1913.

3. Keeping Events in Order

Number the statements below 1, 2, and 3 to show the order in which the events took place.

_____ a. William Mulholland had the idea for the Owens River aqueduct.

_____ b. Los Angeles acquired water rights in the Owens River Valley.

_____ c. William Mulholland became superintendent of the Los Angeles Water Department.

4. Making Correct Inferences

Two of the statements below are correct *inferences,* or reasonable guesses. They are based on information in the passage. The other statement is an incorrect, or faulty, inference. Label the statements C for *correct* inference and F for *faulty* inference.

_____ a. The Owens River was bigger than the Los Angeles River.

_____ b. The Owens River was the closest river to Los Angeles.

_____ c. Water from the Owens River flowed downhill to Los Angeles.

5. Understanding Main Ideas

One of the statements below expresses the main idea of the passage. One statement is too general, or too broad. The other explains only part of the passage; it is too narrow. Label the statements M for *main idea,* B for *too broad,* and N for *too narrow.*

_____ a. Los Angeles first received water from the Owens River in 1913.

_____ b. Los Angeles, like other large cities, needed water to expand.

_____ c. William Mulholland was responsible for bringing new water to Los Angeles.

Correct Answers, Part A _____

Correct Answers, Part B _____

Total Correct Answers _____

The members of the U.S. cabinet act as advisors to the president. They are the heads of the major departments of government. Most are given the title of "secretary." They serve at the pleasure of the chief executive, although the Senate must approve their appointments. Unless they step down for some reason, they may hold their jobs for as long as the president is in office.

The cabinet has no direct control over changes in the law or decisions made by the government. How much power the members wield depends on their importance to the president. Some presidents prefer to seek advice from close personal associates rather than their cabinet appointees. On the other hand, some presidents have asked their most trusted friends to accept jobs in the cabinet.

George Washington named the members of the first cabinet in 1789. There were only four of them: the secretary of state, the secretary of the treasury, the secretary of war, and the attorney general. Over the years, as the country grew, managing this huge nation posed ever-greater challenges. The government met these challenges, in part, by increasing the size of the cabinet. The first secretary of the interior, for instance, was named in 1849. This person oversees the country's natural resources, national parks, and historic sites. Since 1903, the secretary of commerce has focused on domestic business matters as well as trade with foreign countries.

The composition of the cabinet can reflect current concerns of the American people. In 2002, for instance, the year after attacks on Washington, D.C., and New York City, Congress enacted legislation to create the Department of Homeland Security. The new agency takes over responsibilities from some other departments and oversees new projects. Similar changes have occurred in the past, when large departments have been broken into smaller ones. In the year 2002, the cabinet had 15 members.

All members are supposed to have equal status. Two positions, however, can exert great influence in government. One is that of attorney general. As the country's "top lawyer" and head of the Department of Justice, this person is often one of the most visible members of the cabinet. The secretary of state also has a high public profile and is considered the chief cabinet member. This person must work closely with the president on a day-to-day basis to build good relations with other nations.

Reading Time _____

Recalling Facts

1. The members of the U.S. cabinet
   - ❑ a. serve at the pleasure of the Congress.
   - ❑ b. are the heads of major departments of government.
   - ❑ c. exert direct control over the government.

2. The secretary of the interior is responsible for
   - ❑ a. the country's natural resources and historic lands.
   - ❑ b. the interior walls of the White House.
   - ❑ c. trade with foreign countries.

3. In 2002 there were
   - ❑ a. 4 cabinet members.
   - ❑ b. reductions in the number of cabinet members.
   - ❑ c. 15 cabinet members.

4. The composition of the cabinet
   - ❑ a. can never exceed 15 members.
   - ❑ b. reflects current concerns of the American people.
   - ❑ c. must always include the same department heads.

5. In 2002 Congress enacted legislation to create the
   - ❑ a. Department of Justice.
   - ❑ b. Department of Homeland Security.
   - ❑ c. Bureau of Indian Affairs.

Understanding Ideas

6. For a cabinet member to "serve at the pleasure of the chief executive" means that he or she
   - ❑ a. can be dismissed by the Senate.
   - ❑ b. cannot be fired.
   - ❑ c. must resign at the end of the president's term in office.

7. Additions to the president's cabinet over the years reflect the
   - ❑ a. personalities of presidents.
   - ❑ b. political party changes in Congress.
   - ❑ c. development of the nation.

8. From the passage, one can infer that
   - ❑ a. a president should consider carefully the appointment of cabinet members.
   - ❑ b. a president should select a cabinet based on the composition of the previous cabinet.
   - ❑ c. selection of cabinet members should be left to Congress.

9. The fact that the secretary of state is the chief cabinet member suggests that
   - ❑ a. each president establishes a new ranking of cabinet members.
   - ❑ b. building good relations with other nations is important.
   - ❑ c. the chief cabinet member is chosen by the other members.

10. Which of these sentences best expresses the main idea?
    - ❑ a. The first cabinet was named by George Washington in 1789.
    - ❑ b. The Executive branch includes the president's cabinet.
    - ❑ c. Cabinet members serve as advisors to the president.

Janet Reno: First Woman to Become U.S. Attorney General

George Washington named the first attorney general of the United States. More than two hundred years would pass, however, before a woman, Janet Reno, would hold that position.

Reno is the daughter of newspaper reporters and the oldest of four children. She attended public school in her home state of Florida and was a champion debater in high school. Reno majored in chemistry at college and then graduated from Harvard Law School, where she was one of only 16 women in a class of 500. She later worked for the Florida House of Representatives, in the state attorney general's office, and in private law firms.

In 1978 Reno was elected Florida's state attorney. She focused her attention on the problems of youthful offenders and drug-related crime. She pursued parents who failed to make child-support payments and was also a strong advocate of gun control. The voters showed their admiration by returning her to office four more times.

In 1993 Janet Reno was confirmed as President Bill Clinton's attorney general, a position she held until he stepped down from office at the end of his second term. Reno received both criticism and praise for the way she managed the many challenges she faced during her time at the Department of Justice. A courageous woman, she held staunchly to her beliefs.

1. **Recognizing Words in Context**

   Find the word *staunchly* in the passage. One definition below is closest to the meaning of that word. One definition has the opposite or nearly the opposite meaning. The remaining definition has a completely different meaning. Label the definitions C for *closest*, O for *opposite or nearly opposite*, and D for *different*.

   _____ a. feebly

   _____ b. hungrily

   _____ c. firmly

2. **Distinguishing Fact from Opinion**

   Two of the statements below present *facts*, which can be proved. The other statement is an *opinion*, which expresses someone's thoughts or beliefs. Label the statements F for *fact* and O for *opinion*.

   _____ a. George Washington named the first attorney general of the United States.

   _____ b. Reno was a courageous attorney general.

   _____ c. Reno was both criticized and praised as attorney general.

3. Keeping Events in Order

Number the statements below 1, 2, and 3 to show the order in which the events took place.

_____ a. Bill Clinton chooses Reno as his attorney general.

_____ b. Reno is criticized for decisions she makes while at the Department of Justice.

_____ c. Reno serves five terms as the Florida state attorney.

4. Making Correct Inferences

Two of the statements below are correct *inferences,* or reasonable guesses. They are based on information in the passage. The other statement is an incorrect, or faulty, inference. Label the statements C for *correct* inference and F for *faulty* inference.

_____ a. Reno has devoted much of her professional life to politics.

_____ b. Reno was regarded as a productive state attorney in Florida.

_____ c. Reno left politics at the end of President Clinton's second term.

5. Understanding Main Ideas

One of the statements below expresses the main idea of the passage. One statement is too general, or too broad. The other explains only part of the passage; it is too narrow. Label the statements M for *main idea,* B for *too broad,* and N for *too narrow.*

_____ a. Reno is one of many outstanding women in U.S. politics.

_____ b. Reno was confirmed as attorney general of the United States in 1993.

_____ c. Reno started out in Florida politics and then became attorney general of the United States.

Correct Answers, Part A _____

Correct Answers, Part B _____

Total Correct Answers _____

ANSWER KEY

READING RATE GRAPH

COMPREHENSION SCORE GRAPH

COMPREHENSION SKILLS PROFILE GRAPH

ANSWER KEY

1A	1. b 2. a	3. b 4. c	5. a 6. b	7. a 8. a	9. b 10. c	
1B	1. D, O, C	2. F, O, F	3. 3, 1, 2	4. C, C, F	5. B, M, N	
2A	1. a 2. c	3. a 4. b	5. a 6. b	7. a 8. b	9. c 10. c	
2B	1. D, C, O	2. O, F, F	3. 1, 3, 2	4. C, F, C	5. B, N, M	
3A	1. a 2. b	3. a 4. b	5. b 6. a	7. b 8. b	9. b 10. c	
3B	1. C, O, D	2. F, F, O	3. 2, 3, 1	4. C, C, F	5. M, B, N	
4A	1. c 2. b	3. b 4. c	5. a 6. b	7. b 8. b	9. c 10. b	
4B	1. C, D, O	2. O, F, F	3. 1, 2, 3	4. F, C, C	5. M, N, B	
5A	1. c 2. b	3. c 4. c	5. a 6. b	7. c 8. b	9. c 10. b	
5B	1. O, D, C	2. F, F, O	3. 3, 1, 2	4. C, F, C	5. N, M, B	
6A	1. b 2. b	3. c 4. a	5. c 6. b	7. c 8. a	9. b 10. a	
6B	1. D, C, O	2. F, O, F	3. 1, 2, 3	4. C, C, F	5. B, M, N	
7A	1. c 2. a	3. b 4. b	5. a 6. b	7. b 8. c	9. a 10. c	
7B	1. D, O, C	2. F, F, O	3. 2, 1, 3	4. F, C, C	5. B, N, M	
8A	1. a 2. b	3. b 4. c	5. a 6. a	7. c 8. b	9. c 10. b	
8B	1. C, D, O	2. F, O, F	3. 3, 2, 1	4. C, F, C	5. B, M, N	
9A	1. b 2. c	3. a 4. c	5. b 6. a	7. c 8. b	9. c 10. a	
9B	1. O, C, D	2. F, F, O	3. 3, 2, 1	4. C, C, F	5. N, M, B	
10A	1. c 2. a	3. c 4. b	5. a 6. b	7. a 8. a	9. a 10. c	
10B	1. C, O, D	2. O, F, F	3. 3, 1, 2	4. F, C, C	5. B, N, M	
11A	1. a 2. c	3. b 4. a	5. c 6. a	7. b 8. a	9. b 10. b	
11B	1. C, D, O	2. F, F, O	3. 3, 2, 1	4. C, F, C	5. N, B, M	
12A	1. a 2. c	3. b 4. c	5. b 6. b	7. c 8. a	9. c 10. b	
12B	1. D, O, C	2. O, F, F	3. 1, 3, 2	4. C, C, F	5. M, B, N	
13A	1. b 2. c	3. b 4. a	5. c 6. b	7. c 8. a	9. b 10. c	
13B	1. C, O, D	2. F, F, O	3. 1, 2, 3	4. F, C, C	5. N, B, M	

14A	1. b	2. a	3. c	4. c	5. a	6. a	7. b	8. a	9. b	10. c
14B	1. O, C, D		2. F, O, F		3. 3, 2, 1		4. C, F, C		5. M, B, N	
15A	1. c	2. b	3. c	4. a	5. a	6. c	7. b	8. b	9. a	10. c
15B	1. C, O, D		2. O, F, F		3. 1, 2, 3		4. F, C, C		5. N, M, B	
16A	1. b	2. a	3. b	4. b	5. c	6. c	7. c	8. b	9. a	10. a
16B	1. O, C, D		2. F, F, O		3. 2, 3, 1		4. C, C, F		5. N, B, M	
17A	1. b	2. c	3. a	4. a	5. a	6. c	7. b	8. a	9. a	10. b
17B	1. O, D, C		2. F, O, F		3. 1, 3, 2		4. F, C, C		5. M, N, B	
18A	1. c	2. b	3. b	4. a	5. c	6. b	7. a	8. b	9. c	10. b
18B	1. C, O, D		2. F, F, O		3. 3, 2, 1		4. C, F, C		5. N, B, M	
19A	1. a	2. b	3. b	4. a	5. c	6. b	7. c	8. c	9. a	10. a
19B	1. O, D, C		2. F, O, F		3. 2, 3, 1		4. F, C, C		5. M, N, B	
20A	1. c	2. a	3. c	4. c	5. b	6. b	7. c	8. a	9. a	10. b
20B	1. C, D, O		2. O, F, F		3. 3, 1, 2		4. C, C, F		5. B, N, M	
21A	1. b	2. b	3. c	4. a	5. c	6. a	7. c	8. c	9. b	10. b
21B	1. D, O, C		2. F, O, F		3. 2, 1, 3		4. C, F, C		5. M, B, N	
22A	1. b	2. a	3. c	4. a	5. c	6. a	7. c	8. a	9. b	10. b
22B	1. D, C, O		2. O, F, F		3. 2, 3, 1		4. F, C, C		5. B, N, M	
23A	1. a	2. b	3. b	4. c	5. a	6. b	7. a	8. a	9. c	10. a
23B	1. O, C, D		2. F, F, O		3. 2, 1, 3		4. C, C, F		5. B, M, N	
24A	1. b	2. a	3. b	4. c	5. b	6. b	7. b	8. c	9. a	10. a
24B	1. D, C, O		2. F, O, F		3. 2, 3, 1		4. C, F, C		5. N, B, M	
25A	1. b	2. a	3. c	4. b	5. b	6. c	7. c	8. a	9. b	10. c
25B	1. O, D, C		2. F, O, F		3. 2, 3, 1		4. C, C, F		5. B, N, M	

READING RATE

Put an X on the line above each lesson number to show your reading time and words-per-minute rate for that lesson.

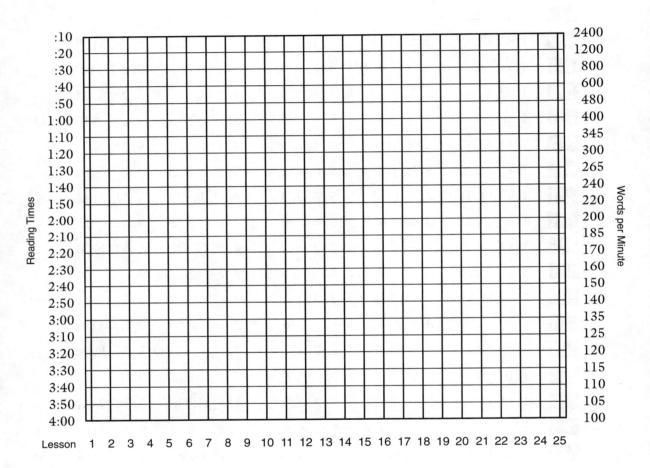

COMPREHENSION SCORE

Put an X on the line above each lesson number to indicate your total correct answers and comprehension score for that lesson.

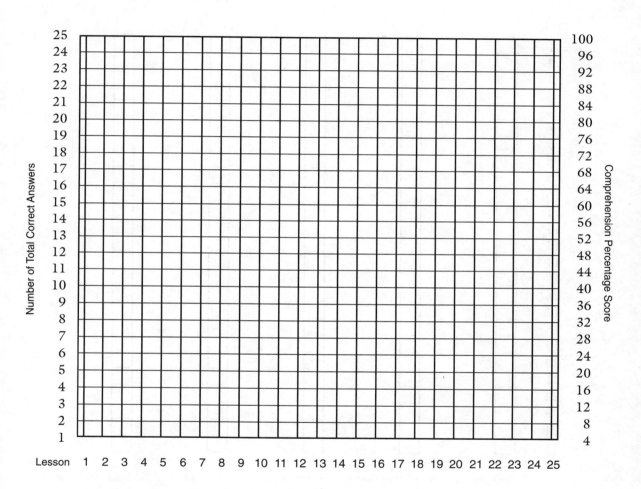

COMPREHENSION SKILLS PROFILE

Put an X in the box above each question type to indicate an incorrect reponse to any part of that question.

Lesson	Recognizing Words in Context	Distinguishing Fact from Opinion	Keeping Events in Order	Making Correct Inferences	Understanding Main Ideas
1					
2					
3					
4					
5					
6					
7					
8					
9					
10					
11					
12					
13					
14					
15					
16					
17					
18					
19					
20					
21					
22					
23					
24					
25					